BUDDHA ON THE BACKSTRETCH

Sports and Religion Series

Edited by Joseph L. Price

Eric Bain-Selbo, *Game Day and God: Football, Faith, and Politics in the American Religion*
Craig A. Forney, *The Holy Trinity of American Sports: Civil Religion n Football, Baseball, and Basketball*
Joseph L. Price, *Rounding the Bases: Baseball and Religion in America*
Marc A. Jolley, *Safe at Home: A Memoir of God, Baseball, and Family*
Robert J. Higgs and Michael Braswell, *An Unholy Alliance: The Sacred and Modern Sports*
Allen E. Hye, *The Great God Baseball: Religion in Modern Baseball Fiction*
Joseph L. Price, editor, *From Season to Season: Sports as American Religion*

Also, *The International Journal of Religion and Sport*, edited by Christopher Anderson and Gordon Marino

MERCER
UNIVERSITY PRESS

Endowed by
TOM WATSON BROWN
and
THE WATSON-BROWN FOUNDATION, INC.

BUDDHA ON THE BACKSTRETCH

THE SPIRITUAL WISDOM OF DRIVING 200 MPH

Arlynda Lee Boyer

MERCER UNIVERSITY PRESS
MACON, GEORGIA

MUP/H782

First Edition.

Books published by Mercer University Press are printed on acid free paper that meets the requirements of American National Standard for Information Sciences—Permanence of Paper for Printed Library Materials.

Mercer University Press is a member of Green Press initiative (greenpressinitiative.org), a nonprofit organization working to help publishers and printers increase their use of recycled paper and decrease their use of fiber derived from endangered forests. This book is printed on recycled paper.

Library of Congress Cataloging-in-Publication Data

Boyer, Arlynda Lee, 1969-
Buddha on the backstretch : the spiritual wisdom of driving 200 mph /
Arlynda Lee Boyer.
p. cm.
Includes bibliographical references and index.
ISBN-13: 978-0-88146-174-9 (hardback : alk. paper)
ISBN-10: 0-88146-174-1 (hard : alk. paper)
1. NASCAR racing. 2. Automobile racing—Religious aspects—Buddhism.
I. Title.
GV1469.25.N37B69 2009
796.720973—dc22
2009021720

CONTENTS

Acknowledgments	viii
Foreword	xiii
Introduction: Why NASCAR? Why Buddhism?	1
Chapter 1: A Bit about NASCAR	8
Chapter 2: A Bit about Buddhism	17
Chapter 3: Meditation and Racing	32
Chapter 4: Flow	46
Chapter 5: Mindfulness	62
Chapter 6: Impermanence	80
Chapter 7: Patience, Endurance *(Kshanti)*	93
Chapter 8: Discipline, Energy, Effort *(Viriya)*	106
Chapter 9: One-pointed Concentration	115
Chapter 10: Equanimity; or, That's Racin'	124
Chapter 11: Accepting Death, Embracing Life	138
Postlude	148
Appendix A: How Dale Earnhardt Made Me a Better Buddhist: An Education in Stillness from a Legend of Speed	153
Appendix B: Some Buddhist Lists	158
Bibliography	165
Notes	169
Index	179

This book is dedicated to the Boyer family, to the Rogauskas family, and to my cherished friends. If I am wise, it is because you have taught me.

ACKNOWLEDGMENTS

This book grew out of a "what now?" moment. I had just finished in second place as a contestant on *Jeopardy!*, taking home a pleasant but not life-changing $2,000. I had the lead going into the final round and knew the answer for dead certain. The question asked who Jesus had called "whited sepulchers." I immediately thought, "Pharisees. No, wait, that's too easy."

Those last five words did me in. I spent the next thirty seconds talking myself *out* of the right answer and into putting down something more difficult, more obscure—and completely incorrect (I answered, "Who were Sadducees?"). So here's a hint—if you're ever on *Jeopardy!*, don't overthink the final answer.

However, I did learn a great Zen lesson from Maggie Speak, a contestant coordinator. In giving the players tips, she told us that if we got a question wrong, we would do well not to brood over it or let it get us off our rhythm. Instead, we needed to shake it off and move on quickly. To illustrate her point, she quoted a line from the Burt Reynolds movie *Gumball Rally.* A character gets into his race car, breaks off the rearview mirror, and throws it out the window, saying, "What's behind you doesn't matter."

Had I put down my instinctive answer on the final question, I would have won close to a year's salary, and I would have come home and been caught up in celebrating, basking in my win and thinking about what to do with the money. But what's behind you doesn't matter, so instead, I came home thinking, "What now?"

February was approaching, and with it the Daytona 500. In 2007, race day fell for the first time on the anniversary of Dale Earnhardt's death. I had written an essay back in 2001 as a way of coming to terms with his death. Though I hadn't really made much effort to get it published, I'd always been fond of it. For the first time, it occurred to me that it might make a good commentary for

NPR. At the time, I worked as a grant writer for the American Shakespeare Center (ASC) in Staunton, Virginia, and one of ASC's former board members worked for our local station, WMRA, in Harrisonburg. I sent the essay to Holley Watts to ask her if she thought it was NPR quality. Holley is my next person to thank because she took the essay and ran with it, forwarding it all around the NPR chain of command. Within two weeks, she had not one but two shows interested in it (a rare occurrence for NPR)—the sports show *Only a Game* and *Weekend Edition Sunday.* Karen Givens, a producer with *Only a Game*, and Holley helped me edit the essay, and when it was down to the required length, I went up to WMRA's studios. Karen phoned in while station engineer Dan Easley managed the recording, and together they coached me through my very first guest commentary.

Before the piece aired, I e-mailed pretty much everyone I knew. My boss told me he and his wife sat in front of the radio as if an FDR Fireside Chat was coming on, not even going outside to get the Sunday paper for fear they would miss a moment. Another couple of friends only got my e-mails after the fact, but both were listening to NPR that morning and recognized my voice. My husband and I set the alarm and lay in bed snuggled under a down comforter (since it was a morning in February and our old house has questionable heat at best) listening to my commentary.

I'd taped an episode of *Jeopardy!* and been an NPR guest commentator in the span of three weeks. I thought that would pretty much be that, and I would go back to my usual routine. But Monday morning, I came into work and found an e-mail from this book's editor waiting for me. Joe Price asked if I was interested in expanding the essay into a book. As you can see, I said yes, and the full version of the essay I edited and read for NPR is in the back.

That's how *Buddha on the Backstretch* came to be. Some of the people I thank might not even know that they helped this book come into being, but they did—so to Maggie at *Jeopardy!* and to Karen, Holley, Dan, and Bob Malesky at NPR, thank you.

My sister Sue Miller will recognize some portions of this book, as they grew out of conversations and e-mail exchanges with her. My husband encouraged me to write the book and continued encouraging me through the whole process, as did his family and mine. Many thanks and much love to them all for cheering me on.

Ralph Alan Cohen, my former boss, is a scholar who loves a good book and a good book-writing project. He was unstinting in his support and infectious in his excitement for me. The ASC deserves special thanks as well. Because I got the essay on NPR through an ASC board member, and also because I loved my job, the company's mission, and all my co-workers on the stage and off, I asked NPR to announce me as "Arlynda Boyer, a grant writer with the American Shakespeare Center in Staunton, Virginia." Had I not done so, it's unlikely that Joe Price would have been able to track me down so quickly. We might never have crossed electronic and radio paths at just the right moment, and so without ASC this book might never have been.

The American Shakespeare Center has built the world's only re-creation of Shakespeare's Blackfriars Playhouse, the first indoor playhouse in the English-speaking world. There and on the road, our two troupes of actors perform Shakespeare as he himself might recognize it—with the lights on, taking "two hours' traffic of our stage" literally, and with the audience on three sides. This frees us from the nineteenth-century "fourth wall" convention of acting and creates instead a community inside the playhouse. Audiences find that Shakespeare wrote them into the action as English troops, Roman crowds, or Danish witnesses to a corrupted royal house. Thus, those who are engaged in acting a play and those who are engaged in hearing and seeing a play create together a communal space of the imagination.

I go on about this because the results of ASC's approach are extraordinary. If you ever have a chance, you should see a show by ASC, either at the Blackfriars in Staunton or at one of their touring stops around the eastern half of the country, and you will see what I mean. I also go on about it because I love these people. They are talented, kind, and funny people who have given themselves to nonprofit classical theatre when almost any other job would provide more money. But they value what we are creating in terms of Shakespeare scholarship and staging practices over any job pushing papers around for an out-of-sight multimillionaire CEO. Every one of them expresses Right Livelihood in action, and every one of them also cheered me on and supported me as I wrote the book. I would like to say a heartfelt "thank you" to everyone in the Resident Troupe, the Touring Troupe, the "box office troupe," and the "administrative troupe" at ASC, especially Gail May, Brent Bussey, Kristie Dillon, and Sandra Murphy.

That brings me to the book's publisher, Marc A. Jolley, and editor, Joseph L. Price. First, I thank them both for the Mercer University Press series on sports and religion. Without it, this book would not have had a home. They steered me to early readings on sports and religion that influenced and refined my thinking. Their writings and those of other authors in the series show that sport at its purest is about living up to one's highest ideals, no matter what arena one plays in or what type of equipment one uses.

Joe's editing was outstanding. He was a sensitive editor, but one with an unfailing eye. I was glad that it was he who mentored me through this process, and I was always touched by his genuine praise and support.

I also gave the manuscript to my longtime friend John Jones to read. I knew John would read it with his usual warmth, wit, and intellect and that he would approach it both as an ideal reader and as a friend. His comments strengthened the book still further, and it is his work as a professional photographer that graces the jacket.

Asking John to photograph me for the jacket photo was a no-brainer. He photographed my wedding to James, and he seems to be the only person in the world talented enough to make me photogenic. Thanks, John!

A quick and only slightly ironic thanks goes to the crew at the FCP poker forum for giving me altogether too many reasons to procrastinate when I didn't feel like researching or writing. I spent a lot of lovely hours there that were supposed to have been spent elsewhere. But where else would I have encountered the profound statement, "When ten people tell you your head is on fire, it might be time to look in a mirror"?

Most of all, I thank my husband and best friend, James Rogauskas—not only for this book but for everything in the past twenty years. I love you.

If I have left anyone out, I apologize sincerely, and if there are any mistakes in the book, they are mine alone.

Staunton, Virginia
October 1, 2008

FOREWORD

When the Mercer series on Sports and Religion was conceived several years ago, expectations abounded about promoting studying the intersections between established religious traditions and sports, the attitudes or policies of religious communities and congregations with respect to sports, and the interpretation of sports as religion or, at least, as a quasi-religion. Near the top of the list of anticipated projects were studies about muscular Christianity, Jewish sports organizations, Asian martial arts, and ancient games rooted in spiritual exercises, like the Olympics and the Mayan ballgame. While initial books in the series featured fans' devotion to various team sports, a shortcoming in the series list became apparent. Speed needed to be added to our lineup. Absent from the series roster was work on the sport fastest growing in American popularity in the latter half of the twentieth century: auto racing.

Given the popularity of NASCAR that now extends well beyond its Southern roots, I began to scan conference programs, anthologies, and journals looking for prospective authors with a penchant for stock car racing and an enthusiasm to reflect seriously on the spiritual connections with the sport. I had expected to solicit projects on NASCAR's commanding appeal, its intertwining with Evangelical Christian ministries, or its history emerging out of moonshiners modifying stock cars to outrun sheriffs or of others drag racing on the sandy Atlantic beaches of North Florida.

I certainly did not expect that the burst of enlightenment about motor sports would come from a transcendent voice—at least one remotely transmitted—expressing a Buddhist oracle. What a paradox: that NASCAR, which originated in a Southern culture suffused with Calvinistic Protestantism, could be explained so well by a non-materialistic religious perspective that originated in Asia. Yet such a revelation about NASCAR interrupted my otherwise ordinary February Sunday morning in 2007. During my drive to sing in a magnificent Presbyterian choir 30 miles from my home, I tuned, as usual, to my local public radio station to hear NPR's *Weekend Edition* and heard Arlynda Boyer deliver a sensitive and profound Buddhist reflection commemorating Dale Earnhardt's death, the sixth anniversary of which was fast approaching. Her commentary proved more spiritually enriching than my worship service later that morning. Her insights into the spiritual nature of her grief and her understanding of the demands and allure of the motor sport itself were astute. She engaged my attention and appreciation in ways that NASCAR friends of forty years had been unable to achieve. She experienced and articulated the complex dimensions of spiritual fascination with stock car racing, such as the liminal thrill of always turning left at speeds around 200 miles per hour. Using a Buddhist lens, she shed light on the American mechanical sport of speed that constantly taunts death. She identified how self-awareness and its corresponding keen sense of presence characterized Earnhardt's competitive drive, and she remarked on his expressions of compassion and joy off the track.

I was fascinated by the searing character of her reflection. Traveling at a fraction of the speed of NASCAR's drivers, I scrawled a mental note of Arlynda's name and affiliation. Later that day I Googled the information, and sent her an appreciative inquiry. The rest, like the list of winners at Daytona, is now history; and like their accomplishments, Arlynda's feat is noteworthy. After a few email exchanges about the possibility of her developing a more thorough Buddhist reflection on "the wisdom of NASCAR," she revved up her research engines and read more than eighty books about the history and heroes of auto racing, works on sports and religion, and studies of Buddhist thought. Then Arlynda drafted and passed her competition, producing *Buddha on the Backstretch*, for which she surely gets the checkered flag.

Her literary voice is as vibrant as her recorded delivery on NPR. And in *Buddha on the Backstretch* she offers reciprocal insight into the world of NASCAR and the practice of Buddhism in one of the most imaginative and impressive works that I have encountered in my exploration and analysis of the intersections of sports of religion during the past twenty-five years. Not only does the work succeed in exploring the world of NASCAR and explaining many of its wonders, it also provides an engaging introduction to Buddhist perspectives and practice. Her chapter on mindfulness—which I shared with a specialist in Buddhist studies, with a convert Buddhist practitioner, and with students in one of my introductory classes—garnered rave reviews from all audiences.

Simply, *Buddha on the Backstretch* is a contemplative work that brings insight and joy to multiple audiences. It makes a riveting contribution to the series on Sports and Religion, to fans of NASCAR, and to students, scholars, and practitioners of Buddhism.

—Joseph L. Price
Editor, Sports and Religion Series

INTRODUCTION

WHY NASCAR? WHY BUDDHISM?

If you cannot find the truth right where you are, where else do you expect to find it?[1]

When you come upon a book about the intersection of NASCAR and Buddhism, one question likely leaps to mind: Why? Thirteenth-century Zen master Dogen provides as good a short answer as any: "If you cannot find the truth right where you are, where else do you expect to find it?" The longer answer is that I grew up in the South, a lifelong NASCAR fan. When I was no more than four or five, I remember my father watching *Wide World of Sports* to see the brief highlights of each race. I remember him pulling for Richard Petty. Later, he liked Harry Gant, a driver beloved of older fans because his greatest success came well after he was forty. Gant taught fans to never give up, and it was then that I had my first stirrings of realization that, with all the victory and defeat and struggle and risk and goals, NASCAR was a pretty good way to learn about life.

As for me, from my very first race in Bristol, Tennessee, I decided that I loved Dale Earnhardt, a fiercely competitive then-newcomer who wouldn't take no for an answer and would as soon wreck as finish second. He was tearing up the sport, and he was loved and hated by equal numbers of fans. No one was indifferent to Dale Earnhardt, and in that unbridled passion I found my hero. He turned out to be a pretty good way to learn about life—and death—too.

As NASCAR fans know, racers are a breed apart—disciplined, dedicated people with intense focus, the patience and spirit to endure years of struggle for a single chance at glory, the will to endure pain, a matter-of-fact acceptance of death, and, ultimately, a passion for living on the edge, a deep understanding of life that as these drivers age lends them a certain unflappable, dryly funny wisdom.

I became a Buddhist about ten years ago. Gradually, it dawned on me that the practice's dedicated teachers, its monks and nuns deep in intense training, with their laser focus on enlightenment, their serene acceptance of death, and their infectious joy, reminded me of someone: race-car drivers. While Buddhists talk of one-pointed concentration, drivers talk of going into a corner three-wide at nearly 200 miles an hour and how effectively that tends to focus the mind. Where Buddhist teachers speak of developing equanimity, an ability to be at ease with whatever arises, drivers go from the lead to last place with a blown engine, then climb out of the car, shrug, and say, "That's racin'." Just as the Buddha told his first followers to meditate in cemeteries in order to deeply realize impermanence, Dale Earnhardt told a reporter, "You can't worry about tomorrow. Tomorrow may never come."[2]

Buddhist teacher Pema Chödrön notes our habitual desire to avoid unpleasant thoughts and feelings, our ways of distracting ourselves even though these distractions do nothing to make the situation go away nor to make us stronger or better people. Instead, she says, "To stay with that shakiness—to stay with a broken heart, with a rumbling stomach, with the feeling of hopelessness and wanting to get revenge—that is the path of true awakening. Sticking with that uncertainty, getting the knack of relaxing in the midst of chaos, learning not to panic—this is the spiritual path."[3] NASCAR drivers must stay with uncertainty, knowing that no matter how hard they worked or how much they want to win, the outcome of the race is fundamentally out of their hands. They must stay with the pain of driving with broken bones or a pinched nerve, sometimes in such bad pain that they must be helped from their car afterward. They must stay with a car that is "off" or struggling, getting passed by bitter rivals while trying to fix the problem in the thirteen seconds of a pit stop. To drive as Earnhardt did, they must stay on the ragged edge of control, barely hanging on to a car to get the most speed out of it, and for three to four solid hours, they must never once panic. Navigating this complex blend of uncertainty, chaos, and skill, as I argue in this book, is *their* spiritual path. And they reap the same sort of wisdom, humor, balance, and rewards as those who study Buddhism.

Although they do not phrase it in this way, NASCAR drivers engage in an extended form of meditation in the race car, and they experience all the same qualities that Buddhist meditators experience—including single-pointed focus, full presence in the moment, and clarity of thought. Consequently, they share some attitudes with Buddhists, such as doing their best in every moment but without becoming attached to specific results. They also share an ability to simply let each race go as soon as it's over, not to chew over the past but to move on easily, to understand the cyclical nature of luck, and to accept outcomes as outcomes without adding great amounts of storyline or emotion to them. They accept death, and through that achieve a deeper, richer joy in living. Finally, they acquire a hard-won wisdom from their uniquely American, uniquely southern, uniquely exciting, uniquely *fun* spiritual path.

To develop my argument about racing as a spiritual path, I will first explain a bit about NASCAR and Buddhism, then more specifically the similarities between meditation and racing. Then I'll examine the qualities that I believe NASCAR and Buddhism share and how some drivers have exhibited those qualities. Although I will use as examples drivers past and present, Dale Earnhardt is my personal template for the quintessential NASCAR driver and my primary example. I realize that for fans of any other driver, this choice is contestable, as though I wrote a book about baseball that only considered the New York Yankees. In truth, I consider the other drivers just as enlightened (or potentially enlightened) as I consider Dale. Part of the reason I use him is sheer familiarity. A Harris poll from January 2000 found that ninety percent of Americans knew who Dale Earnhardt was, and he ranked third as the most widely recognized sports "team," behind only the Yankees and the Dallas Cowboys.[4]

Another reason is that before his death, Earnhardt had reached an age where he had begun to reflect on his storied life and career somewhat philosophically. He had a direct way of speaking about the philosophical angle of racing that few other drivers, besides perhaps Richard Petty, have managed. And he had simply done more interviews—thousands more—than other drivers, leaving a much greater wealth of material from which to draw. Finally, since Earnhardt was a racer's racer, what is true of Earnhardt is generally true of most other drivers as well.

I should also say that, of course, I *do* understand that NASCAR drivers are not Buddhists. For the most part, they belong to the Baptists and other branches of evangelical Protestantism (with the notable exceptions of the Allison family and Juan Pablo Montoya, who are Catholic). Earnhardt himself was a devout Lutheran (to this day, many people do not know that he tithed, or gave ten percent of, his multimillion-dollar income to the Lutheran Church). I am not arguing that drivers should become Buddhists or that Buddhism is the natural path of a NASCAR fan. I am simply pointing out similarities that I have seen from being a Buddhist

NASCAR fan. Additionally, I am making the case that, approached correctly, racing is a spiritual path, and drivers and fans might benefit from considering it as such. By seeing how a popular sport can illustrate spiritual principles, you may learn how to look at anything in life and find the transcendence within it, to realize that every element of life can teach us if we approach with the curiosity of a student.

There is a complex, theological way to explain the matter, articulated by Peter Feldmeier in his reflection on spirituality and sexuality:

> A good way to engage the issue is to attend to a natural law that has become a dictum of the spiritual life: *quidquid recipitur ad modem recipitur recipientis* (whatever is received is received according to the mode of the receiver). This has a twofold meaning, and both are important. First, it means that God moves and transforms us according to our own capacity and our own way of being. Second, it implies that what we know of God and the way we engage God has to correspond to who we are; that we engage our spiritual lives as human beings, dependent on our human make-up.... In the end, what we discover about ourselves informs our knowledge of God, even as a keyhole tells us about the key.[5]

Of course, there is also a much simpler way, one that gets at the same meaning as the passage above. I see NASCAR through the lens of Buddhism and Buddhism through the lens of NASCAR because it is my makeup as a southerner and a Buddhist to do so. It is as simple as that. Being a Buddhist helps me understand NASCAR on a deeper, more profound level, and being a NASCAR fan helps bring to vivid life Buddhism's sometimes academic theories.

I also see the two as connected because I see them both as threads in a sort of tapestry, the tapestry of higher consciousness. Humanity has always sought states of higher consciousness and transcendence. Consider that seeking as the creation of a tapestry, and you will see threads of religious ecstasy, vision quests, hallucinogenic drugs, bungee jumping, moving to the woods to live in a hand-built cabin, meditation, sports…dozens of differently colored threads, all woven into a tapestry that depicts our attempts to transcend day-to-day life. If you look carefully, you can track the threads, seeing where they wind together to make a pattern or where they disappear for a while and reemerge. And once you do so, you will see how easy it is to show how any two of those threads belong in the tapestry, to take them out and weave them together in order to show how well they match and complement each other. NASCAR and Buddhism may be two very distinct threads, but it is my aim to weave them together, to give you a new way to see and appreciate both.

My ultimate intention is not that you become a Buddhist, nor is it that you become a NASCAR fan. There is a Buddhist saying: "When the student is ready, the teacher will appear." I seem to have acquired the gift of being a natural student. I look at everyone I admire, from my boss, to drivers I've never met, to Buddhist teachers, to William Shakespeare, and I wonder, "What is it that this person knows about life that I do not yet know?" I examine their actions and their words carefully to get the answer. They are all my teachers, and I have learned far more about life than my own experiences alone might have taught me. My goal is to leave you asking the same question of all the people *you* admire: What can I learn from this person about life?

Moreover, I want you to realize that there is spirit in all things. All the paths we take in life have the ability to mold our hearts. One of my newest passions is poker, and I could have written much the same book about poker and Buddhism, because poker players must master flow, clarity of mind, patience, and letting go of bad luck in exactly the same way that race-car drivers do. When we truly take the attitude of students, all things can be our teachers. How much we learn from any hobby, any job, any person all depends upon the attitude with which we approach that learning opportunity. It is my hope that you will come away from this book with a heightened ability to see the tapestry woven by sports and spirituality, a resolve to approach all things with the attitude of a student, and a desire to learn the secret wisdom of all those you admire—in short, as Dogen says, the ability to find the truth right where you are.

1

A BIT ABOUT NASCAR

> [NASCAR racing is] kind of like country music. Nobody likes it except the public.[6]

If you came to this book as a Buddhist, you may be wondering, "What exactly is NASCAR?" Likewise, if you came to this book as a NASCAR fan, you may be wondering, "What exactly is Buddhism?" (I'll get to that next.) NASCAR is simply stock-car racing, the mostly oval-course racing found mainly in the South, with sticker-plastered cars that bear at least a mild resemblance to street cars. Although until quite recently it has flown under the radar of the New York/Los Angeles national media, for millions of Americans it is a consuming passion. It grew in the southern Appalachians, in the 1930s and 1940s, out of a need to soup up one's car to get moonshine past the "revenuers." Moonshiners and other car buffs would boast about their fast cars, then challenge each other to races. To avoid the law, drivers had to stay off the streets; instead, they would race in laps around a field, on primitive dirt tracks that car-loving farmers carved out for them. These fields grew into paved tracks and eventually into palaces of speed like the Daytona Speedway, which seats nearly 250,000 people and has grandstands as tall as a four-story building. The drivers grew as well, from moonshiners and mechanics into professional athletes who routinely race with broken bones and still manage to control 3,400 pounds of hurtling metal with just a flick of the wrist.

To most non-fans, NASCAR stands out for the staggering amount of advertising on the cars and drivers' uniforms, for being (apparently) all white, and for being distinctly southern and working class (a.k.a., "redneck"). The advertising simply underwrites the massive cost of staging the sport—to outfit stables of fifteen to twenty handcrafted cars for each of the forty-three drivers in the field (and many of those cars will be wrecked before the season is over, meaning more cars must be built to replace them); to provide payrolls to attract the best mechanics in the nation; to construct testing facilities and wind tunnels to design the car and squeeze out one more bit of horsepower than your competitors; lastly, to provide sufficient compensation to attract a man willing to put his life on the line each and every weekend. Although sportswriter Jeff MacGregor is specifically talking about the Daytona 500, he ticks off the totality of almost any given first lap when he writes, "Seventy-three tons of cars...pouring color and money onto the frontstretch, 34,000 horsepower from $2 million worth of engines wrapped in $7 million worth of sheet metal...before more than $15 million worth of paid attendance, the urgent messages bought by half a billion dollars' worth of corporate sponsorship. The cars are irresistible, as useless and beautiful as jewels."[7]

The sport is still primarily white, although it is trying to diversify its drivers and crews (and, hence, also its fans). The white men who lead the sport understand that no all-white southern sport will ever again be considered a national pastime, and they are working to draw wider audiences. So far, this effort has paid off with a marked increase in Hispanic drivers, and eventually most observers expect (and hope) that the sport will have its Tiger Woods. Minority drivers have noted difficulties in gaining sponsorship, possibly because companies fear that fans will resent the driver, but in fact the minority drivers say that other drivers and fans seem to welcome them. It is beyond the scope of this book to go into a detailed analysis of the sociological role of NASCAR, which is certainly more open-minded and more flexible than most non-fans probably give it credit for being. As many fans point out, black drivers, female drivers, Japanese drivers, and drivers from several Spanish-speaking countries have all had their turns behind a NASCAR wheel. Driver Jeff Burton, tired of being asked how he was "handling" having Colombian driver Juan Pablo Montoya as a competitor, told a reporter, "I wish we were at a place in our society where we didn't have to talk about Juan Montoya because he's not from here. It's sad that we're not there. It's not a NASCAR issue; it's a society issue. At some point, we've got to get past that. And I'll be damn glad when we do."[8]

As for the charge that NASCAR is "redneck," it is probably still accurate to say that NASCAR is more appealing to southerners and to the working class than it is to many other groups. Fully half the racetracks on the circuit are still located in the Southeast, with a few more only a day's drive outside the South, in Pennsylvania, Delaware, and the Midwest—and this condition of being only fifty percent southern comes after a decades-long effort to expand the sport. The drivers' generally southern and middle-American backgrounds, the pro-working man tone of the advertising, the beer and automotive sponsors, and the festively patriotic Fourth of July atmosphere on most race weekends all combine to reinforce a blue-collar southern appeal. Dom Perignon does not sponsor a race car. Budweiser does.

But none of the regional appeal and class distinctions really explain the visceral, passionate devotion that race fans have to their sport. NASCAR touches upon many elements of American culture: cars, speed, money, death, fame, politics, masculinity, class consciousness, the myth of man versus machine, advertising, capitalism, courage, rugged individuality, proud outsider status, and more. Most books about the sport attempt, by describing the events of race day, to capture the force of its appeal; however, they are fighting a losing battle. Words will never capture the moment when the green flag drops and the rumbling engines let out a roar so powerful that you feel every muscle in your body vibrating to it and your own right foot pressing into the metal bleachers as though on an accelerator.

Part of the appeal is the personal familiarity with cars. Nearly everyone can remember the fastest they've ever gone, usually in detail. Whatever the speed, most people tell the story with pride and excitement, their faces glowing slightly at the memory of danger and exhilaration. We can relate to speed, to the competitive thrill of working our way to the front of a knot of traffic, picking off slower cars. MacGregor writes, "It's hard to imagine...shooting a 59 at Medina. But driving too fast? You did that last night on your way home from work. And you'll do it again tomorrow."[9]

Yet underneath our familiarity with cars and our love affair with speed, steel, and the freedom of the road lies a deep anxiety about machines. We do understand that people die or are maimed every day in cars and that our own lives might be snuffed out in a screech of brakes and a tangle of metal. In the man versus machine myth, we always want the man to win.

Reflecting on this complicated relationship between man and machine, social critic Paul Fussell deconstructs a trip to the Indianapolis 500. His observations are worth quoting at some length, as he is one of the few writers to analyze the sport in this way:

> Indy enacts the ritual taming and dominating of machines, emphasizing the crucial distinction between man and machine, the one soft and vulnerable but quick with courage

> and resource, the other hard and threatening but witless and unimaginative, stupid, indeed. The cars are at Indy so that men can be shown able to dominate them, and the wonder and glory of the dominators is the point. Indy is thus like a great Sunday-morning proclamation of the dignity of man, and no number of discarded chicken bones or trampled beer cans can change that....
>
> A longtime student of the race, Sam Posey, seems to get the point when he considers the pleasure spectators take in identifying themselves with the driver-tamer of the machine. When things go wrong and the crowd sees a driver killed, he says, "They are terribly shocked and extremely depressed. They wish they had not been there." What the spectator wants to see is the machine crashing, disintegrating, wheels flying off, and in the end the man springing out and waving, "I'm okay." "Because that's the moment of the greatest thrill," says Posey. "That's when man has conquered the machine. The machine has bitten back, but the man jumps out laughing and therefore the spectator's dream of immortality is confirmed."[10]

Those who cynically dismiss racing and race fans with people who "just want to see wrecks" have a point, but they fail to understand their own criticism. Fans *do*, in a sense, want to see wrecks, but they want to see them because when a driver emerges from the mangled remains of his high-performance machine—perhaps shaken and bruised but with all his manliness and dignity intact—then fans (and perhaps the driver himself) unconsciously confirm that humanity is still superior to the powerful machines we have produced. In a region where machines have resulted in the disappearance of unskilled jobs, this is particularly gratifying, and in a world where machines perform feats of mathematics and speed of which we are utterly incapable, this weekly victory of man over machine makes us feel a little more certain of our place.

The best attempts to explain the appeal of racing come from writers who discard the blow-by-blow of events to consider the cultural elements at play and how strongly those elements affect us. Even ancient history explains something of NASCAR's appeal: Of the six main types of Roman games, including gladiator combat, by far the most popular and the most frequently staged were the chariot races. Historian Roland Auguet observes, "The craze was universal; it affected children as well as adults, slaves (permitted to watch the races and bet) as well as free men. It did not spare even the cultured.... On race day all Rome was to be found on the tiers."[11]

Like chariot drivers in Rome, today's NASCAR drivers are held up as heroes, men who tame the deadly beast of speed. Dale Earnhardt's death—on the last turn of the last lap of the Daytona 500, a race that had given him legendary heartbreak and joy over the years—was as iconic as his life. He had risen from working-class roots to become the bad boy of NASCAR, the Man in Black. The appeal of the bad boy, though, was his blazing desire to win, his implacable will to get past anyone ahead of him, anyone in his way. Fans admired that drive and focus, and they idolized the way he embodied every element of southern masculinity, from hunting, to country music, to simple honesty, to good manners, to religious observance. In a biographical movie produced after his death, one commentator calls him "a superhero." Yet, moments later, a fan says, "He was one of us." It is that combination of qualities that all fans see in their favorite NASCAR driver—a superhero who is one of us. Your driver may be the kind of guy you could have a beer with, but he also possesses talent of a sort you could never imagine, the talent to go 150 miles an hour, six inches away from another car, for hours, and the talent to do it all faster than forty-two other keenly attuned guys doing the same thing.

The beauty of that sort of "superhero/one of us" combination is that it allows us to believe in the superhero in ourselves. If my driver and I both like the same beer, or the same hobbies, and my driver is a superhero, well, then, maybe I have some as-yet-undiscovered superhero quality too! Perhaps not racing cars, but writing, or skill at playing cards, or keeping the best lawn in the neighborhood. If my driver is like me in hobbies or fondness for a particular beer, then maybe I am like my driver in also having a great, singular talent. I believe this possibility of identification is what fans seek from their heroes—permission to discover greatness in themselves. Buddhist teacher Charlotte Joko Beck says of her teacher, "Two qualities of Yasutani Roshi struck me most deeply. I would say he was luminous and ordinary at the same time."[12] A superhero who was one of us, luminous and ordinary—perhaps this combination is what heroes always are. Before his death, Earnhardt was profiled in this way:

> He has entertained you, has endured boos and insults, has lain in hospitals at times, and has lived at the center of what amounts to a national cult for more than 20 years.
>
> We want our heroes to be like us, only a little better, a little braver, a little bigger. Earnhardt has been a lot better, a lot braver, a lot bigger—for a long number of years.[13]

Just as Earnhardt rose from anonymity to become a legend, our heroes transcend ordinary life, and transcendence is one of the things that NASCAR and Buddhism have in common. By transcendence, I mean the ability to shut off that nagging observer in our heads, the voice that never seems impressed, never forgets about the bills, never stops worrying about how we look to others, whether we have some deadly illness, whether we're losing our hair, how to deal with the boss. We want to be absorbed utterly in something so compelling that nothing else is alive for us in that moment. Sex is, or can be, transcendent. Meditation is training in transcendence. Certainly doing something as dangerous as racing—tempting death—transcends the ordinary.

In NASCAR, which has found a way to package and sell nearly everything, even this transcendence can be bought for a price. At several tracks around the country, various driving programs offer the well-heeled fan an opportunity to become the lead-footed. After training, participants learn to drive a stock car, eventually taking it to speeds of up to 160 miles per hour. And what the more insightful of these participants experiences is an extraordinary set of sensations. It is in this extraordinary experience that NASCAR and Buddhism begin to meet. One fan wrote, "All your worries, all your cares, tomorrow, and yesterday drop away, and you're caught up in the present moment, what one theologian called the Eternal Now. Nothing else matters. And if that ain't religion, I don't know what is."[14]

As research for his own book about NASCAR, sportswriter Jeff MacGregor undertook a driving school experience to see what he felt as he tasted the experience of being a driver. He writes,

> I wonder whether professional racers feel the same way I did when I took the wheel of that car—at once powerful and panicked. Have they had the excitement conditioned out of them? Or is every race a 500-mile freefall into darkness? What about the enlightenment? Do they experience the same sense of high-speed *satori* [a Japanese term for enlightenment], however brief, however bogus, that I did? Or is it just another afternoon struggling for a buck to them, every bit as stuck in their own heads, in the unrelenting Q&A of human consciousness, as I am?[15]

After his experience, MacGregor concludes, "Drive fast enough and you hit life's escape velocity: dead or famous, and you're better off either way. At that speed you are bared to the marrow, stripped of everything human except ambition and want—you become a pure, hard consciousness without love or regret or identity. You are speed itself, simple acceleration, a rushing vector of possibility."[16]

The greater goal of transcendence, though, is to find peace. By passing through the limits of ordinary day-to-day life, we arrive at a place of clarity and wisdom. And for that, I leave the last words to Dale Earnhardt, who once said in his wise and plainspoken way, "I feel at peace out there in a race car."[17]

2

A BIT ABOUT BUDDHISM

> Buddhism does not so much offer things to believe as things to do: a vast array of spiritual practices, ranging from moral precepts that one can apply in everyday life and virtues that one can cultivate, to meditative practices (a profusion of these) which help to develop untapped spiritual resources: faculties like profound wisdom or clear-seeing and an all-embracing, selfless compassion.[18]

The first question one might ask about Buddhism is whether or not it is a religion at all. Theologians, anthropologists, and sociologists have debated the exact definition of "religion" for years. As one noted, everyone knows when they see someone practicing their religion, but it is a slippery task to define precisely which actions or beliefs constitute a religion. For example, if worship of a deity is considered essential to religion, then Buddhism is not a religion, because it has no central god or gods. If having a creation story or an end-times story is an essential component, then Buddhism is not a religion, because it has neither. Yet Buddhism has monks and nuns, which certainly seems religious. It has temples and people who identify themselves as Buddhists when asked their religion. It has holidays and rituals, such as funeral rites and readings of the sutras. So it is clear that, in functional terms, people do understand Buddhism as a religion.

I won't settle the long-running debate over what is or is not a religion here. Buddhism has characteristics that could go either way, defining it as a religion or classifying it as a profound—but secular—practice of self-improvement. What I will do is merely describe the practices and attitudes common to Western Buddhism.

When I speak of Buddhism from here on out, readers should understand that I am referring primarily to Western, or American, Buddhism. Buddhism first came to the attention of Westerners during the early Victorian era, when British explorers brought back documents and artifacts from the Far East. Thoreau and other Transcendentalists embraced the first Buddhist texts translated into English, and one finds references to the Lotus Sutra in *Walden*. After a fallow period, Buddhism was popularized again by the Beats, including Jack Kerouac and Allen Ginsberg, and it remained popular throughout the 1960s and into the present day as Asian Buddhist teachers began coming to the West, some of them fleeing the Chinese invasion of Tibet in 1959. As more and more Westerners practice Buddhism, they have created a distinctly Western faith, emphasizing individualism, equality, and freedom. It is this brand of Buddhism that I am discussing. When asked about what Buddhists believe about this issue or that, I find it difficult to answer, because Theravadins may believe something different from Mahayanists, who believe something different altogether from Zen practitioners or Tibetan Buddhists. But that is no different than in Christianity. Ask what Christians believe of saints or speaking in tongues, and you will get vastly different (and completely contradictory) answers depending on whom you have asked. Because it is the tradition I know best, I am sticking with Western, Americanized Buddhism here.

That said, Buddhism was founded by the historical figure of Siddhartha Gautama, a prince of the Shakya tribe of India, around 500 BCE. According to legend, his parents were given a prophecy at his birth that he would either be a great king or an even greater holy man. Since holy men renounce power and wealth, they had little status, so Siddhartha's father raised the boy in sheltered splendor, hoping to keep him from pondering questions of religion. But on chariot trips outside the palace, the boy saw, in turn, an old person, a sick person, a corpse, and an ascetic holy man. He realized that the vicissitudes of existence happen to all and that holy men practice in order to understand and harness these great energies of life. He left the palace and wandered for several years, at last finding enlightenment in deep meditation and realization. After his enlightenment, he taught for nearly forty years before dying of old age. That's it—the Buddha is not considered a god, not possessed of any magical powers, not supernatural. In fact, immediately after his enlightenment, a man came by and, struck by the Buddha's shining countenance, asked, "Are you a god?"

"No."

"Are you a magical being?"

"No."

"A wizard or a saint?"

"No."

"Then what are you?" the man finally asked.

The Buddha replied, "I am awake."

This quality of being awake is the essence of Buddhism. It means to wake up from the countless ways that we deaden ourselves to the world, the ways we distract ourselves from reality through fantasy, daydreaming, entertainment, and so on. It means to wake up to how we mistake our categorizations and our judgments for reality, not realizing they are but the products of our own chattering minds. It means to wake up to the nature of the world, unburdened by the stories we weave about it, and to wake up to the nature of our own thoughts. Once awake, we see our thoughts and how they can control our moods, our desires, our ideas of reality. And we can consciously steer those thoughts to become more peaceful, kinder, and wiser. The significance of being awake is manifest in the title "Buddha," which was given to Siddhartha after his enlightenment. The name comes from the Sanskrit word meaning "awakened," and in keeping with the way that Sanskrit has left its traces on several English words, the same word gives us the root from which we get "bud," or a flower about to awaken.

To steer all persons to become more peaceful and compassionate, kinder and wiser, the Buddha taught something widely known as the Four Noble Truths. They are as follows:

1. In life, there is suffering.
2. This suffering is caused by desire and grasping.
3. To escape suffering, we must cease grasping.
4. The way to relax and cease grasping is the Eightfold Path.

The Eightfold Path is generally divided into three parts, governing wisdom, ethics, and discipline. The parts of the path that govern wisdom are

1. Right View
2. Right Motivation

These two steps remind practitioners to understand correctly the nature of reality (unencumbered by explanation or our personal storyline—in other words, a spilled ice cream cone on the sidewalk is not a tragedy or waste; it is simply spilled ice cream, no more, no less). This surrendering of storyline is Right View, and Right

Motivation means to hold as our motivation the goal of enlightenment.

Ethical Conduct is comprised of

3. Right Speech
4. Right Action
5. Right Livelihood

These three ideals set out parameters for behavior—truthful speech that is useful, rather than idle chatter; actions that are helpful, unselfish, and do what is necessary in the moment it is necessary; and a livelihood that does not oppress or harm the environment, society, or other people.

Mental Discipline is manifested in

6. Right Effort
7. Right Mindfulness
8. Right Concentration

These final three elements of the Eightfold Path ask us to hone our discipline, to be observant, and not to be lazy. Make the effort to become a better person; be mindful of your thoughts, actions, and speech, as well as of the world around you; and live in harmony with the world by practicing the Eightfold Path—this is what the Buddha asked of his followers.

Although the path is numbered one through eight, each step is not to be completed independently. Rather, all steps should be developed simultaneously, and practicing each step in day-to-day life helps support the other steps, since being mindful of our speech tends to make us more truthful and succinct in it as well (thus, for example, Right Mindfulness reinforces Right Speech).

Readers may notice that none of these practices are overtly religious. The Four Noble Truths and the Eightfold Path are the foundational teachings of Buddhism, and yet there is no explanation of how the world was created, no prophecy about how it will end, and no worship of a supernatural deity. Instead, what Buddhism is about is life here and now, how to be a better person day by day. That focus is one way that Buddhism has spread across the world. For example, in Japan, about ninety percent of people say they practice the Shinto faith. About ninety percent also say they are Buddhists. In America, most polls of religious faith add up to approximately 100 percent since people rarely claim more than one faith. The situation in Japan is so different because Shinto is a faith with gods, creation stories, ideas about the fate of the soul after death, and so on. When Buddhism was moving into the country many centuries ago, the emperor considered whether it was a threat to the indigenous Shinto faith and decided that it was not. Shinto dealt with the soul and the afterlife, while Buddhism was a path for daily living in harmony with one another. The emperor determined that there was no conflict between Shinto and Buddhism; thus, in Japan, religious polls often yield a total exceeding 100 percent since practitioners routinely claim to be both Shinto and Buddhist, with no perceived tension between the two paths.

A truly astute reader might raise the question that if the Buddha is simply a human being who became enlightened through his own effort, can anybody become a Buddha? The answer would be yes, potentially. Author Steve Hagen says that the Buddha "attributed his realization and understanding solely to human endeavor and human ability."[19] There are as many Buddhas—past, present, and future—as there are people willing to undertake such a heroic effort to see deeply into the nature of life and mind. Many people in the West might think that Buddhists worship Buddha, an understandable mistake given the term "Buddhist" and our own cultural background of monotheistic worship. However, it is worth noting that in the Far East, there is not really a word that translates as "Buddhist." Practitioners are called "people of the way" or those "on the path." Where Buddhism is widespread, it is understood that the Buddha is not a figure to be worshiped, but a human being (a superhero, but one of us; luminous, yet ordinary) whom his followers seek to emulate.

Another thing that the Buddha taught was the dharma. This word is translated alternately as "the way," "the law," "the path," and simply "what is." Dharma encompasses the Eightfold Path, among other things. It both describes reality and also a method for dealing with it. When one's actions are in line with reality, and also when one is behaving according to the Eightfold Path, one is behaving in line with the dharma. The Four Noble Truths are part of dharma. Teachings are dharma, and following the teachings is dharma. In Asia, those who follow the teachings are called, roughly, "dharma-ists," but this term is translated in the West as "Buddhists." The first teaching that the Buddha gave, that of the Four Noble Truths, is called "turning the wheel of dharma." Subsequent teachings are called later turnings of the wheel. The image is one of a Tibetan prayer wheel, a cylinder containing written prayers. As Tibetans pray, they spin these wheels, releasing the essence of the prayers into the wind.

So we have the Four Noble Truths, the Eightfold Path, dharma, and the Buddha himself, all chiefly concerned with how we live in the day-to-day world. If these teachings sound like self-help techniques or psychology to you, you might not be wrong. Those are categories into which Westerners, especially Americans, have often placed Buddhism. But the bottom line of Buddhism—

the basic question—is always, "What makes me a better person, right here, right now?" The goal is to achieve equanimity, or inner peace, and to root all thoughts, words, and actions in that spacious inner ground of peacefulness. Buddhist teacher Joseph Goldstein says of this American Buddhism,

> A genuine Western Buddhism is now taking birth. Its defining characteristic is neither an elaborate philosophical system nor an attachment to any particular sectarian viewpoint. Rather, it is a simple pragmatism that harkens back to the Buddha himself, who pointedly questioned the established tenets of ancient Indian thought. It is an allegiance to a very simple question: "What works?" What works to free the mind from suffering? What works to engender a heart of compassion? What works to awaken?[20]

But this pragmatic approach is not merely the viewpoint of Americans espousing American ideas. This particular emphasis finds its sources in the Buddha's own teachings and in the 2,500-year history of Buddhism across India, China, and Japan. The Dalai Lama, who serves as the head of Tibetan Buddhism, says,

> [Buddhism] remains relevant everywhere, reaching across the boundaries of nationality, language, religion, and culture. At the heart of the Buddha's teaching lies the idea that the potential for awakening and perfection is present in every human being and that it is a matter of personal effort to realize that potential. The Buddha proclaimed that each individual is a master of his or her own destiny, highlighting the ability that each person holds to achieve enlightenment. In fulfilling this aim what we need is compassion and concern for others and not self-centeredness. Whether you are a Buddhist or not, these are qualities that are worth cultivating.[21]

The essence of Buddhism, then, is characterized by a focus on the present moment as opposed to an afterlife, and on individual effort rather than salvation from a divine figure outside of oneself. Its key premise is that the potential for wisdom, or enlightenment, lies buried within each of us and will be revealed to the world only insofar as we make the effort to uncover it, understand it ourselves, and display it in our words and deeds.

While these teachings are distinct from Christianity, there are threads of this philosophy throughout Western culture. Aristotle said, "We are what we repeatedly do. Excellence, then, is not an act, but a habit," which illustrates the idea of Right Action, how we display our level of wisdom in our deeds, and also how we can consciously steer ourselves toward our highest goals. The prolific author Anonymous said, "Be careful of your thoughts, for they become your words. Be careful of your words, for they become your deeds. Be careful of your deeds, for they become your habits. Be careful of your habits, for they become your destiny." That saying merely restates in a Western way exactly what Buddhists mean when they talk about being mindful, particularly the first clause—be careful of your thoughts. In fact, the motto of my alma mater, New College of Florida, sounds profoundly Buddhist: "In the final analysis, each student is responsible for his or her own education." Each person is responsible for his or her own enlightenment as well. Teacher and writer Sharon Salzburg reports that one of her mentors told her, "The Buddha's enlightenment solved the Buddha's problem. Now you solve yours." No one else can do it for you, and you have to figure out for yourself the answer to the great question, "What works?" What works to make you a better person, first in this moment and then in the next moment and then in the one after that? The essence of Buddhism is about finding and practicing the ever-changing answer to that lifelong question.

A few more Buddhist terms should be defined here. "Suffering," named in the First Noble Truth, is actually the translation of the Sanskrit word *dukkha. Dukkha* is almost impossible to translate fully. "Dis-ease," in the sense of a lack of ease, might be a good translation, because *dukkha* not only involves the suffering of grief or back pain or having your car stolen; it also includes the more profound meanings of subtle sensations, such as a wistfulness or a faint tugging of realization that perfection isn't forthcoming. Imagine someone gave you a fancy, expensive crystal vase, and your first thought was, "Oh, it's lovely! But how am I going to dust it?" That's *dukkha*, the small instant letdown, the bursting of the balloon. Or imagine lying with a lover, wishing that the moment could last forever. The sense of wistfulness and faint sorrow that lies underneath that wish is *dukkha*, the knowledge that the moment won't—and can't—last forever. Perfection isn't quite possible, and to know that is "suffering." This explanation makes clear what the Second Noble Truth is getting at: we suffer because we want the vase to be perpetually dust-free, because we want the moment with the lover to last, because we, unrealistically, want life to be perfect. Grasping at what we want and attempting to flee from what we don't want—but know will eventually happen anyway, like dust and having to get out of bed—is the cause of suffering. The opposite of *dukkha* is *sukha*, which means "ease," and the goal of meditation and Buddhist practice is to find the *sukha* in a world filled with *dukkha*, to be at peace or at ease among the discombobulated and distracted. In these cases, the solution is the Third Noble Truth: simply to cease grasping. When we fully accept that the vase will have to be carefully dusted, the "It's lovely!" is undiluted. When we are comfortable with the fact that the moment with the lover is sweet in part *because* it is temporary, then the moment can be fully savored. And the Fourth Noble Truth is a set of techniques that we can use to help us cease grasping.

Another set of concepts is nirvana and *samsara.*[22] Nirvana is enlightenment, sometimes thought of as a place that enlightened beings go. *Samsara* is its opposite, the world of striving and suffering, greed and envy. However, for Buddhists, such sets of opposites are examples of "dualistic thinking." By freezing concepts into "either/or," we fail to see the possibilities of "both/and." We do not realize that what we think about the concepts, such as "these are opposites," can never be as big or as all-encompassing as the concepts themselves (in turn, the concepts are never as big as reality itself). Instead, Buddhists think in terms of interpenetration, the idea that one concept goes through and into another. To put it as the Buddha did, *samsara* IS nirvana—because without the reasons to practice that *samsara* offers us, we would never find nirvana. Moreover, once we gain some level of realization, we understand that although the world might be *samsara,* we can hold nirvana in our minds and embody it in our actions and words, thus filling the world (*samsara*) with nirvana. Or, in Elizabeth Barrett Browning's charming phrasing, "Earth is crammed with heaven."

Lastly, there is the Buddhist concept of emptiness. This concept is not the somewhat depressing "lack of everything." Rather, it is a notion of emptiness that holds all possibilities simultaneously, like the universe before the Big Bang or like a newborn baby. To be "empty" in the sense that Buddhists understand it is to be free, free from thoughts and concepts, free from expectations and judgments, free from labels and demands. It is empty in the sense that a blank slate is empty, waiting without judgment for anything at all to be added to it. Writers recognize this as "the terror of the blank page," where the page stares back at us, and we stand at the intersection of filling it with brilliance and filling it with drivel. But for those who do not experience this as "terror," emptiness is a vast liberation, a state in which all possibilities are available to us, a state more like purity or innocence or readiness.

Emptiness is also a concept that some have called nihilistic, although I think they are misunderstanding the notion. But it does mean recognizing that our actions are simply done and they fall away. My action is writing a book. A driver's action is racing his car. On the other side of the world, a farmer's action is plowing his field. An aid worker's action is feeding a hungry person. We do the actions, hopefully as mindfully and excellently as we can, and they are simply added to the billions of actions that take place in the world in this one brief minute. Sixty seconds from now, there will be a whole other group of billions of actions. However, the emptiness of our actions is no reason to despair, and certainly no reason to stop acting. We do our actions as perfectly as we can, and they have whatever impact they have, but we do not delude ourselves into thinking that we alone are making the world go round.

I define these terms because they raise a few interesting points. Some readers might point out that NASCAR drivers are enmeshed in the *samsaric* world. They do not practice racing to achieve enlightenment; instead, they race for trophies, for millions of dollars, for fame, and for bragging rights, all ego-centered reasons.

That is somewhat true. As a Tibetan proverb says, "Everything rests on the tip of motivation." Wisdom is not the motivation of NASCAR drivers, so should their racing be considered a spiritual path?

I believe it can be, and often is. Some drivers race for the love of the sport, and view all the rest as simply bonuses (and when they do, other drivers respect them as "true racers"). Moreover, while it is common to avoid behaviors that Buddhists call "hindrances" on the path, such as eating meat (which involves killing), drinking to inebriation, or committing sexual misconduct, there are some sects that seek out precisely those behaviors. Avoiding them is one path to enlightenment, they say, but *defeating* them in direct combat is another path. This method is known as Tantric Buddhism. Its practitioners train for many, many years in traditional Buddhist paths before undertaking the arduous practices of a Tantrist, but once they are on that path they eat meat, drink, and have ritual sex. Some tourists are startled by Indian temples that are, rather famously, covered with sculptures of people copulating—these are temples of Tantric devotion. Although they do not train in Buddhist practices, race-car drivers are similar to Tantrists in that they go directly *through* their intense desire to win, their desire for fame and trophies, and by doing so they arrive, perhaps not at emptiness or equanimity, but at a certain state of grace where they have a more expansive view of life and realize that although for many years they gave racing their all, their most intense effort and their strongest passion, in the end it was never the most important thing in the world.

Ultimately, Buddhism is about the here and now, and what practices one can undertake to perfect this moment, and the one after that, and the one after that. It is an unending process of asking yourself, "Where is my mind right now? Am I living up to my fullest potential right now?" As Joseph Goldstein writes, it is first and foremost concerned with the question, "What works?" Never mind dogma, never mind what I believe about the creation or the ultimate fate of the world (one of which is long past and the other of which is most likely long after my death). Rather, what works *now?*

In fact, my favorite Zen story is about a woman who sought out a Zen master and explained that she was very determined to achieve enlightenment. "Are you sure?" the Zen master asked. "Are you willing to give yourself over completely to seeking it?" When the woman assured him that she was, the Zen master immediately turned into a demon that attached itself permanently to the woman's back and stayed there for the rest of her life, screaming endlessly, "Now! Now! Now! Now!"

I like the joke-like nature of this story, but also the serious meaning behind it. Buddhism is a rigorous practice. Ideally, we question ourselves thousands of times a day, catching our thoughts as they form and steering them again and again toward our highest aspirations. I have found that, in practice, focusing on our highest aspirations and training our thoughts to flow there naturally simply becomes a habit. Even when such behavior is a habit, though, there is still an endless parade of moments in which we begin all over again, catching the next tumbling thought.

Buddhism is a solutions-oriented path. While practice leads to a natural flow in our thoughts and actions, merely feeling happy is not the goal. Rather, the goal is to put our realization into effect in our lives, not simply on display at major holidays or in front of others, but moment by moment by moment, every day. Translator and commentator Glenn Wallis notes, "In place of the theory, belief, faith, and adherence to dogma that many other traditions assert as essential to participation in a religious life, here we find prescriptions for actual practices.... What would it mean, for instance, to live 'relaxed amid the anxious'? What would the actual, *lived* effect be? The claim...is that the effect would be 'ease,' *sukha*, the opposite of *dukkha*, pain. As simple a concept as that may be, you cannot think your way to it."[23] His point is that it is easy while reading about Buddhism to say, "Yes, yes, I get it." But you cannot merely think your way to enlightenment. If you believe you have, not only are you deluded, but you are also clinging to a concept rather than living an actual experience. Furthermore, you may trumpet your supposed enlightenment loudly without ever embodying any kind of compassion or understanding that others can witness. So, instead, you must put the teachings into practice and then practice them tenaciously for quite some time. You must *do* it, not just say it or think it. One Buddhist wisely observes, "Like with everything else in the Buddhist tradition, this notion [of enlightenment] is useful as a verb and harmful as a noun."[24]

That elegantly simple idea of "useful as a verb, harmful as a noun" raises the final point: for Buddhists, the proof is always in the pudding. What you embody moment to moment is what you are. As the proverb says, "Character may be manifested in the great moments, but it is made in the small ones." In the next chapter we will consider how meditators and NASCAR drivers put their respective paths into practice.

3

MEDITATION AND RACING

"The Kingdom of Heaven is within you."—Luke 17:21
"Look within; thou art the Buddha."—Buddha
"He who knows himself knows his Lord."—Muhammad
"Atman [man] and Brahman [god] are one."—Hindu tradition[25]

The goal of meditation is to see one's thoughts as they form and to disengage from the usual weight and credence we give them. It sounds simple, but in reality it is very difficult. If you try to sit for a couple minutes and notice each thought as it occurs, you will realize how many thousands of ideas flit through your mind each day: *This is boring. Am I doing this right? I'm supposed to clear my mind—oops, does that count as a thought? I'm stiff. It's a little chilly in here. As soon as I'm done with this, I need to see to the bills.* It is easy enough to clear the mind for a few seconds, but these mundane little distractions begin to intrude almost immediately. They are not dangerous, psychotic thoughts; they are merely the normal everyday thoughts that we all have, and probably *should* have, in order to manage our lives. So why do Buddhist practitioners meditate in order to clear their minds? Why is the existence of these rambling, mundane thoughts a problem?

The problem is that these thoughts are, as mentioned in chapter 1, "the unrelenting Q&A of human consciousness." That relentlessness is the problem. I have come to believe that, for some people, this level of existence is where they are happy. These quotidian, everyday thoughts are soothing to them, and should they ever be absent, a kind of subconscious terror encroaches that begs to be calmed with a television, an iPod, or cell phone conversations that consist primarily of, "Oh, nothing much. You?" When I see people mindlessly glued to such distractions, I wonder if they are afraid to be alone with their own thoughts. I suspect rather a lot of them actually *are* afraid, fearing that their thoughts will be sad or creepy, or, worse yet, boring.

But other people are dismayed by the relentless chatter of what Buddhists call the "monkey mind," because it leaps like a monkey from branch to branch with no destination in mind and chatters loudly without meaning. Macbeth laments of life, "It is a tale told by an idiot, full of sound and fury, signifying nothing." These people suspect that if that chatter would only slow down or go away for a while, there would be something far greater underneath it—maybe the novel they've always dreamed of writing or maybe a sense of peace and contentment.

That is the goal of meditation—to quiet the monkey mind and to disengage from it, partly in order to free up the potential lying underneath (although most ideally the practice is not goal-oriented—"no gaining idea," as Zen teachers say). The disengaging part, giving less credence to our thoughts, comes from the power that they can have over us. Recall for a moment an incident that made you very angry or very impatient. Think for a moment about what led up to it, how thoughtless the other person was, how hot or brittle or tight or hard-edged the feeling was, how long you were upset afterward.

Spend a few minutes with thoughts like this, and you will notice that you are becoming angry or agitated. Spend a few minutes thinking of a sad incident, and you will become depressed. Yet nothing in the outer world has changed. Your thoughts alone altered your mood. We give thoughts the power to effect this change by giving them all the weight of reality itself.

But what is a thought? Does it have mass? Can it even be located in the brain? It is a will-o-the-wisp, utterly insubstantial, yet with the power to make us weep or rage, the power to alter our whole day—as you know if you have ever woken up "on the wrong side of the bed." We disengage in order to take back conscious power over ourselves, to guide ourselves not according to the whim of our leaping, tumbling thoughts, but according to our ethical and spiritual aspirations. To do so, Buddhist practitioners meditate, watching their thoughts as they form and pass.

The basic instructions of meditation are simple: sit up straight, whether lotus position or in a chair; close your eyes (advanced meditators do not close their eyes, but it is easier for beginners to do so); and pay attention only to your breath. Do not try to force the breath to be even or slow. Simply breathe naturally, and clear your mind. For a beginning meditator, the easiest way to quiet thoughts is to count breaths or simply to say to oneself, "In," on the in-breath, and "Out," on the out-breath. If you stick to saying "in" and "out" with the breaths, the random flow of thoughts slows down, compared to the torrent that tends to gush forth when you are silent.

However, the thoughts are still there, and after a moment they will begin to assert themselves, in between the "ins" and "outs." For me, they appear sort of as cocktail party chatter—I can hear the general hubbub of thoughts passing through my mind, but they are in the background, and I can't quite make each out individually (nor do I try). Thoughts may appear more insistently, and the practice then is simply to label each one "thinking." You might specify, "thinking my knee hurts," "thinking I'm bored," "thinking I'd like to move." What happens is that you are already establishing some distance between yourself and your thoughts. You may even think, "wishing I were rich," "imagining I'm having sex with a movie star," "thinking this whole meditation thing is stupid." Even in thinking that meditation is stupid, you are beginning to see that thought as merely one thought among other random thoughts, not as an absolute truth. You are not reacting to it blindly, but letting it rise and pass away without acting on it. You are no longer giving it the full weight of reality.

"This kind of practice," says Buddhist practitioner Ken McLeod, "requires an effort that is simultaneously gentle without being soft and unyielding without being hard."[26] There is no point in judging our thoughts as they come, thinking that anger is a "bad" thought and love is a "good" thought (remember the concept of emptiness that I discussed before—thoughts are empty, and to assign them a quality or moral status is merely to wrap your personal storyline around them, to encumber them with a false substantiality). There is also no point in judging ourselves for having thoughts, saying, "This is meditation, damn it! My mind is supposed to be empty!" One student complained to his teacher that as soon as he sat down to meditate, his back hurt, his mind nearly leapt out of his skull, and his thoughts swirled like a cloud of gnats. His teacher smiled and said, "Sounds just like my meditation!" The point is not to "do it right"; rather, the point is simply to watch all of that happening, without judgment, and repeatedly to bring yourself back to the breath. The practice is gentle in the way that there is no pressure, but it is not soft in the sense that we simply sit there chasing our thoughts into daydreams, worries, sleep, or wherever they lead. We have the discipline to return again and again to the starting point, to the breath.

Although meditation has immediate calming and de-stressing benefits, it takes some time for us to begin to see the more profound benefits of spacious awareness (which is a sense of being aware of all things without being affected or encumbered by them) and centeredness, or equanimity. Unfortunately, many people try meditation a time or two, for a few minutes at a stretch, announce dismissively that "it doesn't work for me," and abandon the practice in favor of more entertaining pastimes. Teacher Ajahn Chah writes,

> When you begin to cultivate the serenity of...meditation, don't make the mistake of trying once or twice and then giving up because the mind is not peaceful. That's not the right way. You have to cultivate meditation over a long period of time. Why does it have to take so long? Think about it: How many years have we allowed our minds to wander astray? How many years have we *not* been doing [meditation]? Whenever the mind has ordered us to follow it down a particular path, we've rushed after it. To calm that wandering mind, to bring it to a stop, to make it still, a couple of months of meditation won't be enough.[27]

Our goal is to strip ourselves of the stories that we tell ourselves about reality in favor of reality itself, clear and unadorned, to strip ourselves of our narrow web of likes and dislikes, goods and bads, in favor of spacious, magnanimous acceptance. One proverb says, "The person of the way travels light, and lets no opportunity to further lighten his luggage slip by."[28] To travel mentally light, free of the complex, exhausting web of judgments, reactions, and preferences that Buddhists call discursive thought (and the rest of us either call life or simply fail to recognize), is as exhilarating as sprouting wings and taking to the air.

To catch one's thoughts—to strip oneself of distractions and entertainment, to abandon our stories—that is not a small or an easy task. And, as noted, it is one that renews itself with each passing moment. While we eventually move toward more skillful habits, this practice never becomes completely automatic. If it seems to, then we are coasting on a level we understand rather than continuing to dig for fresh, new insights. In *One Dharma*, his book about Western Buddhism, Joseph Goldstein says, "The teachings are simple, but they are not always easy. We quickly discover that, as with any great endeavor, they require energy, commitment, and perseverance. It's not the kind of effort that forces or expects things to happen. Rather, it's the effort to persevere through the innumerable ups and downs of the path. We need to keep going and continually begin again."[29]

What makes this practice worth the effort is the freedom, relaxation, and sense of ease that comes with this clearing away of mental undergrowth. To someone who has never attempted Buddhist or similar practice, it is almost unexplainable. To that person, it sounds like unending work, like rigid, neurotic self-control, like relentless effort. What it is instead is a discipline that is anything but rigid, one that accepts failure from time to time. After all, we can't catch and direct *every* thought, so we have to accept failures hundreds of times a day (honestly, but without recrimination) while still retaining enough kindness and warmth toward ourselves to keep making the effort to be happier and wiser. It is a freedom that comes from a clear, uncluttered mind and an open curiosity toward new people or ideas, willingness to accept things on their own terms rather than trying immediately to pigeonhole them in our preconceived world. To quote Goldstein again,

> As we face the inevitable difficulties and challenges of working with our minds, the temptation will always be to look for some easier way, some other teacher or method. This misses a crucial point in practice: difficulties are part of the path. After

> some time...I began to appreciate the strength that comes from extending beyond the boundaries of comfort zones. Given my own deep-seated inclination toward ease and comfort, a mantra that in times of choice helped me remember the possibility of extending limits was "Choose the difficult."[30]

It may be unpleasant in the short term to "choose the difficult," but in the long run you will always wind up liking yourself better, going further, and respecting yourself more if you do.

All of the Buddhist talk of one-pointed concentration, clear-seeing wisdom, meditative techniques, and managing one's thoughts can seem rather foreign to many Americans. Henry David Thoreau, as American a philosopher as they come, made an observation in *Walden* that strikes me as a way to explain all these concepts. Using Western psychology as his foundation, he asserts,

> By a conscious effort of the mind we can stand aloof from actions and their consequences; and all things, good and bad, go by us like a torrent.... I *may* be affected by a theatrical exhibition; on the other hand, I *may not* be affected by an actual event which appears to concern me much more. I only know myself as...the scene, so to speak, of thoughts and affections; and am sensible of a certain doubleness by which I can stand as remote from myself as from another. However intense my experience, I am conscious of the presence and criticism of a part of me, which, as it were, is not a part of me, but spectator, sharing no experience, but taking note of it; and that is no more I than it is you. When the play, it may be the tragedy, of life is over, the spectator goes his way. It was a kind of fiction, a work of the imagination only, so far as he was concerned. This doubleness may easily make us poor neighbors and friends sometimes.[31]

What Thoreau is talking about is something psychologists call "observer" or "witness" consciousness (or mentality), moments in which we seem to step outside our own lives and watch ourselves as though in a movie. Most of us, I think, have been aware of it at one time or another. But nowhere in Western culture are we trained to use it in any way, or to take control of its flashes of appearance. Thoreau himself merely notes it and moves on. But Buddhism, as I see it, is built around managing this observer consciousness. To gain enough perspective to see our thoughts as mere thoughts, we must be able to step into that observer mentality by a conscious choice. This ability to take control of and utilize our witness consciousness is how we become calm in meditation and achieve equanimity, or inner peace.

At the same time, this internal observer is the very source of the "unrelenting Q&A." In order to transcend reality, we also have to learn how not only to step outside of the observer consciousness, but to shut it down entirely for a while. The trick is learning how to shift our primary awareness from the observer to the observed, as it were, from the spectator in our heads to the doer in our bodies and hearts. This consciously chosen shift of identification is the technique of Buddhism. After learning to manage our minds this way, we begin to advance toward states like egolessness and enlightenment. Ultimately, the goal is to dissolve completely the barrier between observer mentality and our ordinary mentality, so that the mindfulness of the observer becomes united with the absorption of the doer, in a state of grace in which we see all aspects of an event at once, yet are totally focused on just the right action at the right moment. An athlete calls this mental state "playing in the zone." To a Buddhist, it is the state produced by meditation. Andrew Cooper, a writer who examines sports in the context of religion, says, "The name of the game is to set the busy-ness of the mind aside and fully bring one's attention to bear on the immediate task at hand.... There is, in Zen terms, 'nothing extra'—no ego standing apart from the action encumbering it with useless commentary."[32]

The connection to NASCAR in all this explanation of psychological and Buddhist perspectives is that drivers must learn to manage their minds, and that goal is at least as important as managing the car. Minutes before the green flag, drivers "get their game face on" (and by the word "game," the reader can recognize a similar phenomenon in other sports as well). They clear their minds and focus on the task before them, and for this practice most of them value a few minutes of stillness, even if it is only a self-created stillness within the cockpit of the car, tuning out the screams of thousands of fans.

Settling into the right frame of mind is a fundamental step in all sports. It combines both mindfulness and focus, seeing everything, but seeing the goal clearest of all. Old-time driver Fred Lorenzen said of modern-day NASCAR, "There's more money in it and the cars are shinier. But [overall], it's still four tires and a brain."[33]

Lorenzen was right to place his focus on the driver's mind, because that's exactly what NASCAR is—four tires and a brain. Some people say that NASCAR drivers are not athletes, ignoring the physical stamina necessary for racing. But beyond physical stamina are the mental demands that racing places on a driver. Most players in most games spend at least some time on the bench (sometimes more than half the game), and most games move no faster than the speed of human running. But at triple-digit speeds, with only breaks brief in duration that come at unpredictable intervals, a driver must depend on intense, unbroken concentration. To lose one's game face in the car is to invite disaster. Some drivers have even confessed to causing wrecks due to a momentary loss of concentration, as Dale Earnhardt Jr. did when he admitted that during a practice session in his rookie season he was watching his rearview mirror and forgot there was a turn coming up. He hit the wall at full speed and cracked a shoulder blade. While NASCAR officials were fretting about whether his throttle had stuck (the suspected cause of an earlier fatality), he ruefully admitted that, nope, he had merely let his mind wander for a couple seconds—and, at those speeds, a couple seconds is all it takes to miss a turn and crash.

To get the right mindset, one has to have the right motivation. In the end, worldly goals such as trophies, money, or fame count for little, and although those are the rewards NASCAR drivers chase, most of them understand the ultimate emptiness in these material rewards. Drivers and fans make a distinction between "drivers," who race cars for a living, and "racers," who live to race cars. Earnhardt was always considered a racer, and it was a high compliment from his colleagues. It was often said that if an organizer put on a race but said, "Sorry, there's no trophy, nobody in the stands, no championship points, and no prize money to be paid," the only driver to show up would be Earnhardt, and he would be rarin' to go. A few other drivers have merited the term "racer," such as Kenny Schrader and Tony Stewart, both of whom regularly show up at tiny rural dirt tracks to race just for the love of the sport. The motivation of true racers is the love of the sport and the love of competition. Right motivation does not consider how rich or how famous one might become, or that one might prove oneself through racing. Right motivation simply loves the challenge for its own sake.

In an example of the way Buddhism tends to wrap around itself and come back to the same ground, motivation is considered essential because wrong motivation leads right back to the First Noble Truth, suffering. It leads to *dukkha* precisely *because* it is impure, yet Right Motivation, which is a step on the Eightfold Path, leads to nirvana precisely because it is pure. In this vein, Robert Pirsig observes in *Zen and the Art of Motorcycle Maintenance*, "When you try to climb a mountain to prove how big you are, you almost never make it. And even if you do it's a hollow victory. In order to sustain the victory you have to prove yourself again and again in some other way, and again and again and again, driven forever to fill a false image, haunted by the fear that the image is not true and someone will find out. That's never the way."[34] The motivation must simply be the love of the challenge, be it the mountain, the racetrack, writing, playing poker, bike riding, or something else. And in a description of motivation that any race-car driver would appreciate, Pirsig goes on to add, "An adequate supply of gumption is the first and most important tool. If you haven't got that you might as well gather up all the other tools and put them away, because they won't do you any good."[35] Gumption, as any southerner can tell you, accounts for quite a lot. For Dale Earnhardt, gumption was working a full shift at a factory, then coming home to work on the race car until he fell asleep with the wrench in his hand and sleeping under the car until he woke up for the next factory shift. Gumption was flipping his race car several times, but upon discovering that it still ran, jumping out of the ambulance to drive the nearly destroyed car back to the pits, refusing to give up while there was racing still to be done.

The drawbacks of wrong motivation are unwittingly illustrated by Earnhardt's son, Dale Jr., as he writes about his rookie season: "It is a fear of failure that drives me.... Perhaps this is why I am rarely alone, choosing to surround myself with friends and acquaintances as often as I can."[36] He also admits that being a race-car driver is something he has been ambivalent about doing, wanting it but also more or less falling into it as the family business, and with a considerable amount of worry about being seen as the boss's son, whose "ride" was bought and paid for rather than earned. Although his father had also been the son of a racer, he debuted during a period of much less media scrutiny, and Dale Sr. had entered the sport utterly unafraid of failure. He simply threw himself into a pursuit that he loved for its own sake, and the difference in motivation between father and son is clear. Compare Dale Jr.'s comments about his rookie season to his father's comments about his philosophy toward driving and about his attitude once he got in the car: "There are no deep, dark secrets.... That's part of the philosophy my daddy taught me: you prepare that race car the best you can, and you work hard and you run hard and you keep your composure about you, and it'll all work out. You establish your territory. And you always stay cool on the racetrack."[37] Another writer quoted Dale Sr.: "I feel totally relaxed in the race car. I can tune everything else out. In a way, it's my retreat. It's probably the place where I'm most at home."[38]

To establish right motivation and to sustain a clear, focused mind for hours at a stretch—this is how NASCAR drivers behave like Buddhist meditators, and from like actions come like results. A common Zen saying notes, "Enlightenment is always an accident, but some activities make you accident-prone."[39] Having the right motivation for racing helps drivers absorb themselves completely in the act of racing. Fear of failure or desire for material rewards and recognition can leave too much room for the mind to wander dangerously. Likewise, Buddhist practitioners do not meditate in order to look good in their robes or to seem exotic or to sit down and figure out a problem that is vexing them. They set their motivation as enlightenment and meditate in order to begin the process of training their minds. To a practitioner, the mind is like an athlete's body. An athlete trains his or her body for a sport, and a meditator trains his or her mind for practice. Trophies and seeming exotic are not motivations that can sustain us in difficult times—what sustains us is the love of what we do, our passion for it. That is why, for drivers, love for the minute-by-minute, lap-by-lap experience of racing helps them clear their minds and perform at their best, and, for Buddhists, setting aside all goals but enlightenment helps us to clear our minds and focus on the path.

Meditation is beginning to appear as a tool of sports psychologists, leading more athletes to explore meditation's ability to help them maintain the mental focus and discipline they need. NASCAR driver Brian Vickers is the first driver to say that he meditates regularly. His sessions last an hour, and he says he can tell the difference in his daily life as well, in feeling calmer and mentally clearer. He may be a trendsetter among drivers for now, but I doubt that five years from now, or possibly even one year from now, he will still be alone in his practice. Racing is such a competitive sport that whenever one driver discovers a practice that gives him a competitive edge, other drivers copy it immediately. Years ago, most drivers resisted physical training regimens and consulting nutritionists, but as soon as one top driver won a championship while exercising and carefully planning his season-long diet, other drivers got on board. They may have preferred eating glass to eating salad, but their desire to be the best overcame any resistance. They did what they had to do to win, and since Vickers has proven himself a consistent contender for wins, I believe other drivers will take note of his meditation practice and try it themselves.

I believe Vickers would agree that racing is in itself an activity leading to higher consciousness and wisdom. Meditation supports his path, but the path he is on is racing. Similarly, for Buddhists, meditation supports the entire Eightfold Path that helps us shape our thoughts, our words, our deeds, and our understanding. Meditation alone does not lead to higher consciousness, by which I mean wisdom or enlightenment, but the calming and quieting of the mind creates a space where we can still our mental chatter and begin the disciplines that do take us there—whether those disciplines belong to the athletic world, the spiritual one, or the intellectual one. Thus, if we set out with Right Motivation, we will not be distracted by fear, temporal desires, or laziness, but will resolutely still the chattering monkey in our heads and create the calm, focused mind that can embark on a path to enlightenment, a NASCAR title, or whatever meaning with which we imbue our imagined best life, the life in which we become our own luminous, yet ordinary superhero.

4

FLOW

The key point here is that you are in control of how you respond to what happens to you, that is, you are responsible for your own thoughts and actions.[40]

Responsibility is a human quality most often associated with actions. Yet, for some people, it seems to be a radical idea that they are also responsible for their own thoughts. Thoughts (and feelings), they assume, spring up in us from some unknown place, and we go wherever they take us. The thought "I'm hungry" takes us to the refrigerator. Anger takes us to a place we call "angry."

But philosophers, Buddhists, and athletes all recognize the truth of the above quote. Our thoughts and feelings exist solely inside our heads. Nobody puts them there, and nobody can exert control over them except us. As often as we may say, "He made me angry," the fact is that we can control our own emotions and reactions—if we choose to. Philosopher Robert C. Solomon says, "If you look at your emotions and say, 'I will take responsibility for this because it is my doing,' sometimes you will be wrong; but in general, you will suddenly find that you've taken ownership of your life in a way that you hadn't before."[41]

As Solomon points out, and as psychologists Susan Jackson and Mihaly Csikszentmihalyi (who pioneered the concept of flow that we are discussing in this chapter) have studied, the result of learning to observe the mind and steer it in accordance with our athletic ambitions, or our ethical and intellectual ambitions, is that we take ownership of our lives in a most gratifying way. We feel powerful and free, centered in ourselves, and certain of our ability to take on a challenge. This kind of mental preparation and discipline can lead to an extraordinary state of being that Csikszentmihalyi has described as "flow," which can be defined as

> a state of consciousness where one becomes totally absorbed in what one is doing, to the exclusion of all other thoughts and emotions. So flow is about focus. More than just focus, however, flow is a harmonious experience where mind and body are working together effortlessly, leaving the person feeling that something special has just occurred. So flow is also about enjoyment. People associate flow with peak performance...although winning is important, flow does not depend on it, and flow offers something more than just a successful outcome. This is because flow lifts experience from the ordinary to the optimal, and it is in those moments that we feel truly alive and in tune with what we are doing.[42]

In their study of flow and sports, Jackson and Csikszentmihalyi did not examine racing. Nevertheless, their insights about the perception of time and focus during intense sporting events apply precisely to NASCAR. They note that time often feels altered during a flow experience, so that long, endurance-type events seem to the athlete to pass more quickly; in a complementary way, they note that bursts of activity—such as first and goal in a football game or a triple play in baseball—seem to stretch out luxuriously so that the athlete feels he or she can see all the choices, choose the right one, and anticipate an opponent's moves.[43]

Magnifying this experience, NASCAR combines a three-hour endurance event (with in-car temperatures reaching 140 degrees) with bursts of activity (avoiding spinning, sliding cars in the event of an accident) that can unfold at any given moment and require split-second reflexes. Driver Kyle Petty has said that, in racing, time itself feels different, but he did not elaborate on whether it seems faster, slower, or simply more fluid and flexible. Either way, race-car driving seems to be an especially fertile field for examining extended experiences of sports flow, because while Jackson and Csikszentmihalyi say that flow is a rare event, I suspect that drivers actually spend quite a bit of time in a flow state.

Another element of flow is the feeling that even a physically taxing activity has passed easily, leaving the athlete feeling almost refreshed at the end rather than drained. This experience is so common in NASCAR that it is practically a weekly occurrence for one driver or another to get out of his car saying, "Man, I could run another 500 miles, easy." They are not idly boasting or presenting a false front; instead, the drivers who make this comment at the end of a long day genuinely look as fresh as they did before the green flag, delighted with a great-handling car and their own long period of intense focus. This energized yet emotionally calm and easy mental state is the result of the driver having been in a flow state for hours. It is also the mental state produced by the practice of meditation. This similarity is why flow and Buddhism share so many traits in common, and also why I believe that racing and Buddhism share many traits as well. In studying more traditional sports, I think Jackson and Csikszentmihalyi missed the sport that is actually most generous in producing flow.

Apart from a sense of delight and the stretching of time, the most important defining characteristic of flow is mental clarity and concentration and a marked absence—blessed silence—from the "unrelenting Q&A," the observer consciousness that keeps us standing just slightly and painfully apart from our own lives. As noted in the last chapter, stepping into the observer mentality can be a useful meditation technique that helps us learn to see our thoughts merely as thoughts and not as the very definition and creation of reality. Letting go of the constant pressure to judge, to comment, to pigeonhole, to interpret, to *prefer,* is calming and liberating. Just letting our thoughts rise and fall away, to pass without our feeling any need to act on them or even believe them, gives us the first glimpses of what Buddhists call "spacious awareness" or "calm abiding."

In racing, a problem arises and a driver in a state of flow sees it, sizes it up, chooses how to handle it, handles it, and moves on to the next thing, almost instantaneously, without adding a mental commentary on his luck or how problems are the last thing he needs or how much a bad finish will cost him. This calm and clarity is the driver operating in spacious awareness—seeing and acting without commentary or emotional imbalance. In Buddhism, spacious awareness is an attitude attained through meditation and practiced in daily life. A Buddhist absorbs himself or herself fully in each task, does that task with all the perfection they can bring to it in that moment, and then moves on to the next task, letting the first one vanish into the past without clinging to it, thinking, "Did everyone see how well I did that?" One writer jokes that Buddhism is rather like a Frank Sinatra chorus—"do, be, do, be, do."

While we can achieve distance from our thoughts by consciously calling up the observer mentality, I suspect that state of mind is a crude tool for Buddhist practice. Although Westerners might recognize it most easily, it is also dangerously close to that peculiarly American disease of postmodern alienation. Realizing that our emotional commentary and mental discourse are idiosyncratic, and therefore not reality, is not the same as simply not caring or assuming a posture of emotional deadness. If we did that, we would find it virtually impossible to absorb ourselves in anything, much less to approach all our tasks with as much perfection as we can. For instance, Buddhists think of a chore, "This chore is not the annoyance or the inconvenience that my discursive mind wants to make it. Rather, it is simply a task, waiting to be done. And I am simply here, doing it. It exists, I exist, and I do it. No problems."

In Buddhist thought, every concept has "far enemies" and "near enemies." The far enemy of a concept is its opposite, but the near enemy is something that is similar but emanates from the ego rather than from any higher or purer place. The example most commonly given is compassion. Compassion expresses itself as "What can I do to help?" The self is merely a tool, important only for the ways it can provide help. The help is the main offer and the main motivation. Compassion's far enemy is indifference, simply turning a blind eye to those who are suffering or in need. But the near enemy of compassion is even more insidious—pity. Pity expresses itself as "I feel terrible for you." It's all about the self, how the self feels, how important it is that the self makes its feelings known. Notice that there is no offer of help and no setting aside of the ego to get involved or be of practical use. French philosopher and Buddhist monk Matthieu Ricard accurately distinguishes compassion and pity without designating either of the attitudes and actions: "When the self ceases to be the most important thing in the world, we find it easier to focus our concern on others. The sight of their suffering bolsters our courage and resolve to work on their behalf, instead of crippling us with our own emotional distress."[44] In this way, observer mentality and its risk of alienation might be considered a sort of "near enemy" of the equanimity and spaciousness of Buddhism. However, for those who need to connect to Buddhism through Western equivalents, witness mentality may be approached as a neighbor to equanimity, as long as one realizes that the two are not perfectly synonymous.

Compare the Buddhist state of spacious awareness and Ricard's description of what happens when the self is not held as paramount to what Jackson and Csikszentmihalyi say of flow:

> Concern for the self disappears when one is in flow, as do worries or negative thoughts. There is simply no attention left over to worry about the things that in everyday life we usually spend so much time dwelling on. Flow frees the individual from self-concern and self-doubt. Loss of self-consciousness is an empowering characteristic: after the flow experience, the perception of self is stronger and more positive. Relinquishing worries about the self for a period of time is also refreshing and liberating.[45]

Obviously, Jackson and Csikszentmihalyi understand the feeling of being frustrated and hemmed in by the "unrelenting Q&A of human consciousness," and they understand what Buddhist author Andrew Cooper was getting at when he said that the point of Zen is to achieve a state where there is "nothing extra—no ego standing apart from the action encumbering it with useless commentary."[46]

Although the theory of flow was originally influenced by the work of psychologist Abraham Maslow and his ideas of self-actualization and peak experience,[47] it is easy to see how similar the theory is to Buddhist ideas. As noted, the goal in Buddhism is ultimately to merge observer awareness with absorption so that we see our thoughts rising and falling away without undue attachment to them. While we see our thoughts as the fleeting, ephemeral, and insubstantial things they really are, we also engage ourselves totally in each task we undertake, whether it be racing a car or doing the laundry. Moreover, look back at the previous quotation from

Jackson and Csikszentmihalyi and notice how often the word "self" occurs, especially in negative terms—self-doubt, self-consciousness, self-concern. Besides being unrelenting in general, this "ego standing apart" is also interminably, annoyingly navel-gazing—self-involved, self-absorbed, and narcissistic.

So the key element in flow, in Buddhism, and in auto racing is the honing of the mind to quiet our usual mental chatter, to dampen or still for a while our habitual self-consciousness. Why is this principle so vital, and how does one go about doing it?

According to all three practices—experiencing flow, practicing Buddhism, and racing NASCAR—self-consciousness is a hindrance because it is "extra" and unnecessary. Jackson and Csikszentmihalyi say, "no attention left over to worry." Cooper says, "nothing extra, no...useless commentary." Maslow speaks of "submersion of the self." But even beyond being merely unnecessary, self-consciousness is an impediment to absorption. If we are not absorbed, we are distracted, and distraction is not conducive to excellence. Thus, self-consciousness prevents us from achieving excellence. For many people, self-consciousness even prevents them from trying. Many would-be writers have fantasized about authoring the next bestseller, being fawned over and anointed by Oprah, sitting cozily in a mansion spilling their brilliance onto the page, only to find themselves unable to sit down and actually produce a single chapter. First, a Buddhist would point out that money and fame provide insufficient, misdirected motivation—and because the motivation is wrong, it will lead to the suffering of self-conscious paralysis. Flow theorists would say there is too much attention and ego left over to question, to doubt, to procrastinate. A NASCAR driver would probably simply say that there is not enough mental discipline. In other words, you cannot reach flow if you lack the discipline to submerge the self, and you cannot submerge the self if your motivation is all about self-gratification in the first place. Lastly, a Zen master would point you toward a deeper level of honesty and self-knowledge, saying that if you say you want to do something very much, but never manage to do it, then you don't really want to do it much at all—at least, not enough to put forth the necessary effort toward it. Zen masters are great believers in the adage "Actions speak louder than words."

Cooper points out how easy it is for self-consciousness to become neurosis. "When the door of self-consciousness is opened," he says, "the self becomes vulnerable to all manner of mental mischief." Furthermore, Cooper goes on,

> this is particularly disruptive, even debilitating, when the self chases its own tail, so to speak, in a downward spiral of fear, self-doubt, and self-criticism. This dynamic is an essential feature in most neuroses. The agoraphobic panics over going out in public because he fears that going out in public will cause him to panic. The singer is overcome by anxiety about going onstage because she fears that going onstage will cause her to be overcome by anxiety.... The cycle of self-consciousness depletes one's inner reserves of knowledge, intuition, imagination, and mental energy.[48]

The single action needed for achieving what could alternately be termed *samadhi* (meditative absorption), flow, or "game face" is this: concentrate. It is purely a matter of will and effort to block out the ego's rambling soliloquy and give oneself to the task at hand, and it is purely a matter of will as to how much we succeed in doing so. The mind that is producing all this chatter is also the mind that we control, and our intentional desire to concentrate is more than capable of silencing our unintentional chatter, if we exert the effort. We must simply observe the thoughts, recognize the random firings of "check e-mail," "bored," "play a few hands of solitaire," "see what's on TV," and so on as monkey mind chattering away, and while one part of our mind (the ego-based, self-conscious observer) is gushing forth these thoughts, we must engage the quiet, goal-driven part to say, "No, I am not going to follow that monkey around right now. He's not going anywhere important."

This is why the practice of meditation is the foundation of all other Buddhist practices—because meditation consists of simply watching our thoughts, learning to recognize them and their emptiness at the moment they arise, rather than after we've elevated them to reality and rushed off after them for the billionth time. With meditation, thoughts can seem almost like foreign objects in the mind, distinct from us, and they have not the power to compel activity, nor the power to stir up emotional tempests, nor the power to undermine us with daydreams and self-doubt. Once we can see our thoughts clearly and consistently like this, moment to moment, then concentrating enough to reach the flow state is within our reach.

The good news is that it does not take long for this discipline to become a habit. When the chatter has no effect, it begins to dry up, and we develop a stiller, calmer mind more ready to enter concentrative states and more likely to slip into the state of heightened awareness and grace known as flow. Concentration, say Jackson and Csikszentmihalyi, "is a critical component and one of the characteristics of optimal experience mentioned most often. Learning to exclude irrelevant thoughts from consciousness and instead to tune into the task at hand is a sign of a disciplined mind. Being able to exclude all the distracting events happening around your performance is not easy, but it is an important skill to master if you want to experience flow in sport."[49] They also add, "Ultimately, control in sport is not about opponents or external obstacles. It is about learning to discipline a wandering mind, fluttering emotions, an unsteady will. Sport creates the possibility of achieving control over the self."[50] So does Buddhism, and this is my point: Because sport (in this case, auto racing) and Buddhism both promote the same goals, drivers and practitioners can both offer us examples of wisdom in action. Please read that last quotation again, about disciplining a wandering mind, because it is important. This goes far beyond the occasional race-car driver or marathon runner. This is a lesson in how to master life itself, a lesson in how we live when we are at our very best. It is as useful to you and me as it is to any athlete—even more so, since they are trained for it and you and I must stumble upon this lesson ourselves, in our own reading or our own experience.

To some people—perhaps to many comfort-oriented Americans who prefer "choosing the easy" over choosing the difficult and who tend to view self-control with suspicion—the description of gaining control over the self sounds like the rigid "control" of a neurotic. That perception couldn't be further from the case. Neurotic "self-control" is repression. It consists of *denying* the existence of the ego's commentary, insisting, "My mind isn't wandering, my mind isn't wandering, my mind isn't wandering," more loudly and more insistently as it becomes less and less true. Ultimately there is only one end to this kind of effort—a hopelessly unfocused mind and the giving up of the task altogether amid bitter self-recrimination and depression.

Compare that neurotic repression with Buddhist *samadhi* (meditative absorption) and the concentration necessary for flow. Both intentionally acknowledge the wandering mind, the ego that stands apart creating commentary, and then both deliberately say, "I choose not to follow those thoughts right now. I understand that they are there, but I am choosing a different direction." Denying something that you know perfectly well to be true is irrational, nonsensical. But accepting its existence does not make you its slave. Acknowledge the thoughts, and then let them go. Return to the task in which you seek flow. And keep returning, with each breath, and returning again, and in this gently authoritative manner, without harshness toward yourself, but with friendly warmth, you will achieve a mind that is relaxed yet focused.

Preparing for and Finding the Right Circumstances for Flow

Properly preparing for a sports event is a foundational practice for an athlete. Properly observing the mind prior to working with it is a foundational practice in Buddhism. Without laying solid foundations, further progress in either discipline is unlikely. Jackson and Csikszentmihalyi define the most promising conditions for flow as those in which the demands are just slightly above your current skill level. If the challenges are too far above, you will feel intense anxiety and disassociate into the ego-consciousness that gets in the way of absorption. If the challenges are too easy, you will feel bored and escape for entertainment into the daydreams of ego-consciousness again.

In NASCAR, the balance between too hard and too easy is illustrated nicely. Drivers are nearly unanimous in their loathing for practice sessions, test sessions, and tire sessions. All are necessary times they must drive the car in order to shake it down and work out any minor mechanical issues, or when they must run several sets of tires in for a few laps each to give them proper grip on the track surface, or when the team is testing a new setup for the car. Speeds are lower, and the car is often alone or nearly alone on the track. There is no competition, nobody to pass, nobody chasing you, and therefore no flow, no *samadhi*, no joy or high-speed *satori*.

But many drivers also dislike Daytona and Talladega, two of the fastest, most dangerous tracks on the NASCAR circuit. Both tracks have killed or seriously injured well-respected drivers whose skills were thought of as excellent, and both tracks use restrictor plates, which effectively shrink the holes in the carburetor and allow less speed (by allowing less gas into the engine). Restrictor plates tend to equalize all forty-three cars, so rather than stringing out along the whole track, race cars travel in a tight pack, and because of the pack, when one car goes out of control, it usually takes several others with it. For the drivers who are vocal about their dislike of these two tracks, it is apparent that they feel anxiety about racing there. The skills needed are just a little too far above their own perceived skills (although they would never admit that), and they know it will be a long, hot afternoon without the clarity of thought and action they can enjoy at other tracks. Whether they know it or not, they are delineating a fairly precise image of the conditions for flow—not so easy a challenge as test sessions, but not so difficult as four hours trapped in a tight pack of jostling cars.

The practice of "getting one's game face on" is the initial step in preparing for flow. One athlete said, "I've got to be relaxed, but I've also got to be hyped up; it's almost in between—sort of anxious and sort of relaxed. It's a fine line, because if I'm too relaxed, I'm just downhill, and if I'm too anxious, I'm downhill, too."[51]

Dale Earnhardt prepared for a race using similar methods. For a time, before each race, doctors would measure the drivers' heart rates, doing research on the physical demands of racing. Week in and week out, Earnhardt took inordinate delight and pride in the fact that his heart rate was always the lowest. He said he never had butterflies before a race, and scorned those who did. He projected the very image of cool and collected before getting into his race car, a stance that many more nervous drivers found deeply intimidating. By proving that he was calmer than anyone else, he implied that he was better prepared and ready to win before the green flag even fell.

Earnhardt was well aware of this psychological advantage. Typically, before a Sunday race, Saturday is a frantic day of working out last-minute kinks and endlessly tweaking the car. Once, Earnhardt and his team arrived at the track, took a few desultory practice laps, then put the car away and went hunting. The bold move stunned the garage, and all other teams could talk about was how confident he was and how amazing the car must already be. Sure enough, he won the race the next day, and for years after laughed about how he'd really won it on Saturday by going hunting.

But although he always had the lowest heart rate, Earnhardt told reporters nobody was more excited than he was to get the race started. He described himself as being like a kid on Christmas morning every race weekend, waiting all week long for the green flag to fall so that he could get into the race car that gave him peace and be in the place he loved the most—flying around a racetrack. He had mastered the right blend of excitement and calm that lends itself to flow, and I have to believe that his statement about being at peace in a race car indicates that he experienced flow and the fruits of meditative absorption routinely. Noting this excitement that paradoxically leads to calm, and the expertise it takes to arrive at such a moment, Jackson and Csikszentmihalyi cite an old Italian adage: "'Impara l'arte, e mettila da parte' which translated literally means 'learn the art, and then put it aside.' It is good advice not only for artists and craftsmen, but also for experiencing flow in sport: Practice the skills to the point that you can forget you have them. Then abandon yourself to the performance."[52] Earnhardt definitely knew how to abandon himself to the performance.

Flow and Driving While Injured

Although it is not the point of flow to enable an athlete to endure pain, it does create a level of concentration where pain can be transcended. Since I believe that NASCAR drivers experience flow regularly and in far longer lengths of time than most other athletes, it would stand to reason that they are more likely to drive through pain. As it turns out, this supposition is true (although it is also built into the sport's structure). Again, Jackson and Csikszentmihalyi note, "Marathon runners, long-distance swimmers, and cross-country skiers, for example, must draw on enormous reserves of will and stamina to complete their events. And yet, even among these most excruciating ordeals, athletes describe moments when they are able to ignore the pain and enter an effortless rhythm that transforms the agony into ecstasy. Often, athletes refer to such times as 'being in the zone.'"[53] Race-car drivers depend on being constantly, and fully, absorbed in the task of driving. Because the sport's championship system awards points per race, with the annual champion becoming the driver who amasses the most points over the course of a season, it is nearly impossible for any driver to take a week off. No matter how seriously a driver may have been injured in a wreck, the points system (which was originally put in place to deter drivers from sitting out small events and racing only for the biggest purses) demands that he get right back in the car. Backup drivers do not necessarily earn points.[54] In professional team sports, an injured player can take several weeks off to recover while a second-stringer plays his position, and the team is scarcely hampered. NASCAR talks a great deal about teamwork, but when it comes to driving the car, it is a one-person sport, and the lack of a driver cripples the team. There are no second strings.

As a result, drivers fight through even severe pain and injury on a routine basis. A few examples: Harry Gant raced shortly after bruising his heart. Tim Richmond raced—brilliantly—with "pneumonia" (there remains some question about whether he knew at the time that he actually had the AIDS that would kill him a year later). Dale Earnhardt raced with a broken back (not the wisest of his decisions since he felt it break in a late-season wreck and finished the season without telling anyone what had happened) and also started a race two weeks after shattering his collarbone and sternum. Ricky Rudd raced with eyes so blackened and puffy from a previous wreck that he had to tape his eyelids open to keep them from swelling shut. Drivers have raced—and won—with flu, food poisoning, broken bones of all sorts, burns, and even amputation.

In this regard, Ken Schrader takes the driving-through-pain trophy. While Ken was working on his engine one Friday, one of his crew mistakenly turned the ignition. Ken's hands were still deep in the engine, and a spinning belt cleanly sliced off his thumb. His crew grabbed the thumb and rushed Schrader to the hospital, where a doctor looked things over and said, "Sure, we can reattach that. We'll have to completely immobilize the hand for eight or nine weeks. After that, you should be able to get right back to driving."

Schrader thought this over for a moment, and told the stunned doctor, "Toss the thumb. Just bandage me up and get me out of here. I ain't got time to be missing races."[55] Opposable thumbs are nice and all, but racing is racing.

Now, that's not what's crazy about Schrader's story. What is crazy is that every single driver, to a man, thought he had made exactly the right decision. And after this happened on Friday,

Schrader raced on Sunday. After the race, Michael Waltrip pulled alongside and teasingly gave him a "thumbs-up." Schrader responded with an altogether different hand signal. When NASCAR fans say that drivers are a different breed of people, this intensity is what they mean—in wit, in toughness, and in the single-minded dedication to the sport they live for.

5

MINDFULNESS

Do not take lightly small misdeeds
Believing they can do no harm
Even a tiny spark of fire
Can set alight a mountain of hay.[56]

The point of meditation is to clear the mind, silence the internal observer, and concentrate fully on the present moment. Through meditation, the practitioner seeks to acquire the qualities of mindfulness, patience, equanimity, discipline, relaxation, and joy. There are three major elements to mindfulness. First, there is being fully present in the moment. Second, when we practice mindfulness, we pay attention to the little things, being thoroughly conscientious or observant, with a degree of deep absorption in whatever task we find ourselves doing. Finally, mindfulness consists of bare awareness, simply seeing and understanding without adding storyline or emotion.

Mindfulness is simply paying attention to what is real, what is right in front of us now. All of us know how it feels to be driving or walking somewhere and suddenly realize that we have covered a good bit of distance without any awareness of doing so. We had been so lost in our thoughts, even rambling thoughts about nothing in particular, that the last several blocks or miles passed without us noticing them.

Obviously, the intent of mindfulness is to avoid such periods of absent-mindedness. While it may not be immediately apparent why we would want to still the chatter of our usual thoughts, it also may not be apparent why mindfulness is a good thing. After all, I have spent many pleasant hours myself driving down the interstate daydreaming, fantasizing, and planning.

But what was my actual *life* in those moments? It was driving. Not to be mindful is to miss out on the lives we are leading. It is to be at least partially (and sometimes almost wholly) absent from our own existence. How much, exactly, of your life would you like to live only half-present? Most people would say none—or, more honestly, they might say, "the employed part"—but without mindfulness, we are all unconsciously choosing to be absent from our lives, mere spectators when we should be the most active participants.

Mindfulness is full engagement with reality as it is right now, nothing more or less. I have offered this explanation to people and gotten the response, "But that's boring!" (or depressing, or stressful—some answer that shows they are troubled by the prospect). They never seem to realize that they are saying their *lives*, as they live them, are boring, or depressing, or stressful. Of course, that's exactly what they are saying—that they would rather escape into fantasy than to confront their own lives. Then, perhaps, they would see it for what it really is and take the steps necessary to make their lives more exciting, more fulfilling, or more peaceful. Joseph Goldstein has a wonderfully thought-provoking way of addressing this challenge, pointing out how our very language favors daydreams over deep engagement with real life: "It is telling that in English 'disenchanted' [and] 'disillusioned'...often have a negative connotation.... Becoming disenchanted means breaking the spell of enchantment, waking up into a greater and fuller reality. *This is the happy ending of so many great myths and fairy tales.*

Being disillusioned is...a reconnection with what is true, free of illusion"[57] (italics mine).

Mindfulness, as well as all the other qualities that I believe race-car drivers share with Buddhists, is both a practice and a quality that results from the practice. That is, we practice mindfulness in order to have mindfulness. This nature of being simultaneously practice and quality tends to be true of many tenets throughout Buddhism, which goes back to the idea that our moment-to-moment actions are both the ground of our practice and also the visible fruits of that same practice. In Japanese hotel rooms, instead of the Gideon Bible, one finds a copy of the teachings of the Buddha tucked into a drawer. This book says, "Those who seek enlightenment must be careful of their each step. No matter how high one's aspiration may be, it must be attained step by step. The steps of the path to enlightenment must be taken in our everyday life."[58] Unless we practice the mindfulness of observing each thought and action as it occurs, we cannot attain the quality of mindfulness that guides us to enlightenment. Similarly, a person whose practice is peace behaves in ways that emanate peacefulness, making peace both their practice and a quality that describes them.

Furthermore, in Buddhism, establishing distance from our thoughts often means seeing emotion as something we *practice* rather than something we feel. Thus, "The painful thing is that when we buy into disapproval, we are practicing disapproval. When we buy into harshness, we are practicing harshness. The more we do it, the stronger these qualities become. How sad it is that we become so expert at causing harm to ourselves and others."[59] This quotation emphasizes the understanding that rather than being at the mercy of our thoughts and feelings, we are the force that creates them. We practice anger, depression, impatience—honing all of these practices into an entirely unwanted, unintended path of spiritual misery. Or we practice mindfulness, happiness, and patience—honing these practices into a path that brings us joy and lasting inner peace.

The Zen school of Buddhism is particularly focused on mindfulness as a path to enlightenment, and there are numerous anecdotes to illustrate it. One of the most common is the saying, "Before enlightenment: chop wood, carry water. After enlightenment: chop wood, carry water." Before enlightenment, we do our chores with distracted minds, thinking of other things, perhaps thinking that once we are enlightened all this hassle with chores will go away. After enlightenment, we do our chores mindfully; each task is experienced as an absorbing one because we do not have the discursive mind constantly judging it against some scale of whether it is glamorous enough or hip enough to absorb us or whether it should be scorned as "boring." Not surprisingly, chores do not vanish simply because we have attained clarity of mind. Fires don't burn without chopped wood, and rice doesn't boil unless water is put on the stove. But no matter: the chores are beautiful things in themselves because we have the quality of mindfulness and are fully engaged with our lives, as we should be. So when I speak of mindfulness in some places as a practice and in other places as a quality, I am not merely being lazy or confused in my terms. I am using them in a Buddhist sense in which what we feel and the way we behave—our qualities—are our moment-to-moment practice.

Moreover, this quality/practice extends not only to our activities, but also to our interactions with others. When we are not mindful, we may divide our attention between someone we are with and the television set in the room, or we may be busy formulating our responses in our heads while the other person is still talking, so that we are only partially listening. Full mindfulness means giving others our complete attention, listening to every word, and eliminating all distractions. We are fully present for them and fully involved in them, and to others, this mindfulness practice comes across as deeply caring, a true kindness in a world where it sometimes seems everyone is half-listening and keeping one eye on the TV.

For a NASCAR driver, mindfulness consists mainly of noticing the little things and being at one (fully absorbed) with the car. On the track, the slightest bobble of one car can set off a multi-car pileup; drivers must notice the tiniest change of motion or speed in their competitors as well as their own cars. Frequently, some driver will make his way down pit road because one tire doesn't feel quite right. As often as not, there is indeed a tiny cut on the tire, and stopping prevented the driver from suffering a high-speed flat and a probable wreck. Many old-school drivers from the 1950s through the 1970s say they learned to drive barefoot so that they would learn to feel each subtle change in the car through the pedals.

To heighten his sense of being fully absorbed in his car and the race, Earnhardt insisted on wearing an open-face helmet long after the practice was abandoned by other drivers. Part of the reason he did so was his practice of careful observation. One of his most remarkable talents was driving at restrictor-plate tracks like Daytona and Talladega. To drive such tracks successfully, a driver must understand the physics of air flow, called "the draft." Traveling behind another car yields a less turbulent air stream and enables both cars to go faster. Being the lead car means having the least turbulence, because it is driving through undisturbed air. Thus, cars hook up in a "train," several vehicles long. To break out of this line of cars throws a car into turbulence, and the effect on the car is almost like slamming on the brakes. Unless a driver ducks into another line of cars, he will lose ground to the cars still in the draft.

Earnhardt was a legend at both restrictor-plate tracks, winner of more events of that type than any other driver, and often winning in spectacular fashion. Reporters said that he could "see the air." But besides his innate skill in handling the race car, he also had the practice of mindfulness on which he relied. The open-face helmet allowed him to feel the air as it flowed into the car. When it felt right to him, he knew it was time to pull out and go. He also said he sometimes took off his racing gloves and held a bare hand up to the window. Again, when the air felt just right, he ducked out of the train and usually into the lead and the win.

Generally, the forty-three cars in a race travel in two side-by-side trains, and at different moments in the race one line of cars will be faster than the other. When that happens, drivers in the slower line will duck into the faster one, but they almost universally duck into the middle of the line and work their way toward the front by picking off one car at a time.

Earnhardt's most impressive talent was that he almost always waited for a line of overtaking cars to move up nearly to his rear bumper. Then he swung down deftly and became the leader of the faster train. It is a remarkably gutsy move, and a dangerous one, and to this day, no other driver does it routinely. It was pure Earnhardt. Only he could "steal" the train, and he could do it because he could feel the pocket of air beside his car changing as the line approached.

Other drivers talk about horsepower and strategy, but Earnhardt noticed the small things, like tiny shifts in air turbulence, and his mindfulness of what was around him paid off. Shunryu Suzuki says in the classic *Zen Mind, Beginner's Mind,*

"When your mind is wandering about elsewhere you have no chance to express yourself. But if you limit your activity to what you can do just now, in this moment, then you can express fully your true nature, which is the universal Buddha nature. This is our way."[60] This was also Earnhardt's way—to discipline his wandering mind, to focus only on what he was doing in the moment, and to do it with excellence, expressing his true nature as a gifted and daring racer.

Meditation and witness consciousness begin to teach us how to step back and establish some distance between ourselves and our thoughts, to hear them and see them as they pass through our minds rather than simply reacting to them immediately as though they were reality itself. John Snelling describes mindfulness as the process of stepping back from the "ongoing drama," the "waking dream," and the "habit patterns" of our day-to-day lives.[61] Steve Hagen says, "The foolish reject what they see, not what they think. The wise reject what they think, not what they see,"[62] emphasizing non-attachment to our thoughts and a clearer perception of reality, undecorated by our stories about it.

Lama Surya Das, an American-born lama (spiritual teacher), writes, "When the Buddha said, 'We are what we think,' he was asking us to take responsibility for our inner life."[63] Das learned how to take responsibility for his own inner life during years of rigorous meditation practice in India. Watching his thoughts, he realized that "in each and every moment, my mindstream and feeling world was a mixed bag of all kinds of pollutants and obscurations, fears and prejudices, habitual responses and knee-jerk reactions, selective memory, personal storytelling, sharp desires and semiconscious confused longings."[64] Again, just as the meditation teacher laughingly told her frustrated student that his description sounded exactly like her meditation, I think that if we are honest, most of us will realize that our thoughts are often much the same, ranging from cluttered to chaotic.

So mindfulness consists in part of being aware of what we are doing, what is around us, and what is transpiring in our own thoughts. In this regard, Glenn Wallis, translator of *The Dhammapada*, says, "Mindfulness…establishes precisely the proper frame of reference for living one's life in its all, in its fullness, at the very instant it transpires—now."[65] As he points out, the reward for mindfulness is experiencing life in all its fullness, not missing anything by being only half-present. I wrote above that mindfulness consists of three elements: full presence in the moment, absorption, and bare awareness. Obviously, being fully present in each moment leads directly to the idea of being absorbed in the moment. One-pointed concentration is another closely related quality that I believe Buddhists and NASCAR drivers share, and I will explain it more thoroughly later, but mindfulness begins to touch on it in some respects with the second element of absorption. For instance, Charlotte Joko Beck, author of *Everyday Zen*, observed of Mother Teresa, "She was just doing the next thing and the next thing and the next thing, totally absorbing herself in each task—which is what we need to learn. Her life is her work, doing each task wholeheartedly, moment after moment."[66]

Similarly, drivers absorb themselves completely in driving. Dale Earnhardt Jr. said, "Once I'm fully strapped into this harness, I feel as if I'm part of the car—almost as if I'm the heart and brains of this machine."[67] He also observed, "Short-track racing is like walking through a minefield. You have to watch every move and *be completely aware* of what's going on around you. If you give the guy in front of you some room, you'll get booted from behind. You can get bit by a lot of things you didn't have anything to do with starting"[68] [italics mine]. Whether or not the driver universally called "Junior" would recognize it, he specifically names mindfulness as his way of handling the demands of short-track racing. Asked how he remained so calm before each race, his father mused to a reporter, "You see so much more than you used to see. I reckon age does that to you."[69] Clearly, by referring to age, he means "seeing" in the sense of understanding as well as observing.

Concentration is a fundamental part of all athletics. Many athletes would not consider concentration a part of spiritual practice, but simply an element of training not unlike eating right or sticking to a workout schedule. But athletes regularly do the mental work of sports, and much of this work corresponds neatly to the work that Buddhist practitioners do. Athletes train themselves to attain a state of relaxed readiness before an event, and Buddhists sit down to meditation in a state that is alert yet calm. Athletes must shake off setbacks in the course of an event and remain focused on the final outcome, and Buddhists learn to accept setbacks without adding negative thought patterns to them. Finally, athletes learn to focus completely on their event, and Buddhists learn the art of absorbing themselves fully in living moment to moment.

Concentration, according to Andrew Cooper, is as important a part of sport as the rules, the playing field, or a player's skill. He says, "For those playing at the highest levels, the ability to put oneself in a state of heightened concentration—to get 'psyched up,' to 'stay focused'—is as essential as physical ability, technical mastery, and knowledge of the game."[70] He quotes Japanese baseball player Sadaharu Oh, describing his moment at bat: "And in the midst of it, in the midst of chanting and cheering crowds, colors, noises, hot and cold weather, the glare of lights, or rain on my skin, there was only this noiseless, colorless, heatless void in which the pitcher and I together enacted our certain preordained ritual of the home run."[71]

The first two elements of mindfulness are being present in the moment and being absorbed in the moment. Both elements stress paying one's full attention to whatever is happening in the moment. The last element is concerned with the quality of that attention, the type of attention one pays and the internal narrative one experiences.

The last element of mindfulness is bare awareness. This means to observe and attend to reality not only with full engagement, but also to do it without adding our own personal storylines or explanations to matters. When we see "bad" drivers on the highway, we have already altered unadorned reality with our own judgment call, our own emotional reaction, and our own storyline: *This is what a bad driver does; it's not what I do; I don't like this driver; I want this driver to be more like I expect a driver to be*; and so on. And ditto for all the other things we see and immediately describe to ourselves with adjectives. Every adjective is a subjective judgment, a way of stamping the world with your ego, saying, "Here's what I think. It's important because it's not just monkey mind; it's *how things are.*" Unfortunately for us, that certainty is an illusion. Our storylines and judgments are purely subjective. My perfect weather is somebody else's much too hot, and somebody's brisk, energizing day is my much too cold. More importantly, my religion is somebody else's superstitious nonsense, and my politics are somebody's nation-destroying insanity—and if I am not being mindful, I may react to their views the same way.

Not everyone is going to see reality as you do, and if you insist that your personal stories are "how things are," then you have created a world in which everyone who disagrees with you is wrong—an enemy even, because they threaten your worldview.

You want to be "right," and you are so bound up with your reactive mind that you cannot take a step back from your thoughts, either to gain the sense of spaciousness that comes from doing so or even merely to engage reality as it is. Thus, bare awareness, stripped of your habitual personal narrative, is a necessary element of mindfulness and part of the Eightfold Path. On this topic, Lama Surya Das says, "We must accept the givens of a particular situation without projecting upon them too quickly or too clumsily our own passion-driven, reactive list of highly subjective likes and dislikes, goods and bads, rights and wrongs, victories and defeats."[72]

Having explained the elements of mindfulness, I want to show you how mindfulness is key to NASCAR. Rather than citing several unconnected examples, though, I will repeat one driver's story. Dale Earnhardt became a legend, but one day the legend sat down with a couple reporters writing a profile of him, and he recounted a story from his boyhood. Decades before Earnhardt would take his first checkered flag or set his first record, he had already begun the practice of mindfulness that would set him on the path he later achieved.

I also want to note that the stories people choose to tell about themselves are windows to their souls, or at least to their values. Of all the experiences in their lives, certain ones become stories that they tell about themselves repeatedly. Why do they reach for that story? Because something about it resonates for them. It is their way of explaining why they are the type of person they are. Ask anyone for a story about their past. Some people will tell you how tough their early lives were, and they will probably be people who pride themselves on overcoming adversity, perhaps even to the point of dismissing the struggles of others as "not as bad as what I went through." Another person might tell you a funny story about themselves that has become a family legend. That person is likely to value family ties, and his or her story underlines the close knit of his or her family.

For Dale Earnhardt, the following story—about the first time he ever prepared a racecar for his father—resonated for him. It was an experience that shaped him as a person, as a racer's son, and as someone who would one day be a racer himself. His story encompasses all these elements of mindfulness—absorption, being aware of every little thing, and bare awareness. Using rural North Carolina as the focus rather than the ancient Far East as a context, this story also sums up much of what we have considered in this chapter. As you read the following paragraphs, think about how mindfulness is clearly illustrated in all its forms—being fully absorbed in a task, paying attention to the little things, and seeing unadorned reality (in this case, loose bolts) and saying, "Here's what needs to be done," without attaching any judgment to it. Consider how Earnhardt used stories like this one to shape his character. Along this same line of thought, Lama Surya Das asks of Buddhism, "Can we actually live in such a way, not just believing in these virtues but actually embodying and practicing them day by day, hour by hour, minute by minute?"[73] In other words, can we actually practice mindfulness minute by minute, instead of merely believing it to be a nice but impractical ideal? Earnhardt's story makes clear that the answer is yes.

> Dad's racing shop was right behind our house. I always helped him. Even when I was small, I swept the floors. I swept and swept until I doubt there was a speck of dust anywhere. I'd do anything to stay in that shop and be around those race cars.
>
> When I was just a little boy, I knew the difference in tools. I knew a half-inch wrench from a three-quarter-inch before I could say my ABCs.

I think I handed Daddy tools before I ever started to school. I thought I received a promotion the day he let me wash the tools, dry them, and put them away. After they dried, I put them in drawers. Each one had its place. Dad could open a drawer and take out the right tool without even looking.

My brother, Randy, hung around the shop a lot, too, but I think I paid more attention to the cars and what was happening.

I remember the big thing with me was I wanted to be trusted. When I got a little older, I was allowed to wash the race cars and clean out the radiators. Dad was racing on dirt tracks, and keeping the radiators clean was a pretty big job.

On mornings after Daddy raced, I got up before anybody else and went to the race shop. I'd check out the grille, wheel wells, and undercarriage. If there wasn't much dirt on the front of the car, I knew Daddy probably won the race. If the car had red clay sticking to it, chances were good he had finished second or third. He seldom finished any farther back than third.

I'd wash the race car, and by the time I got back in the house, Mother was usually fixing breakfast. If Daddy was up, we'd talk about the race he ran the night before, and then I'd leave for school.

At night, Daddy would build and work on his race engines. I watched closely. I was learning as I went along.

I remember the first important thing he let me do. I was 15 years old, and he had this 427 engine in a 1961 Chevrolet. Those engines were hard on bearings. He won a race at Greenville-Pickens Speedway the first time he ran the big block engine. Then we started having problems with the bearings. We would tear the engine down every week to make sure we were not tearing up anything inside the motor.

Meanwhile, he raced at Columbia, South Carolina, on Thursday nights, Monroe on Friday nights, and Greenville-Pickens Saturday nights. Daddy raced his Malibu with the small-block engine at Columbia and Greenville-Pickens, and raced with the big engine at Monroe.

He worked all week on the car and engine, but did not have time to put the engine back in the car. It was Thursday morning and he had to race at Columbia that night. He looked at me and said, "I'll tell you what I'm going to do. I have a race to run tonight, so I won't be here when you come home from school. The engine we are going to run Friday night will be sitting here ready for you to put in the race car. Put it and the transmission in and bolt it all together. I will check it over tomorrow. I'm depending on you."

I was 15 years old. I said, "Really?"

He said, "Yeah."

I wouldn't do anything to a race car without his permission.

I'll guarantee you I was the happiest and proudest kid at school that day, but I didn't tell anybody about my project.

That was all I thought about in school.

I got home and started to work. I thought about everything. Is that bolt tight? Does this fit?

I put the radiator in and tightened it; then I put water in the radiator and bled it out to make sure there was no airlock.

I finished everything about 10 o'clock, cleaned the tools and took special care to turn off the lights and the oxygen to the welding machine. Then I went to bed and rolled and tossed half the night, worried that I had forgotten something.

The next morning I was washing the car Daddy had raced. He came out and cranked up the car with the motor I had installed. He warmed up the engine and looked to see if I had done everything right. When I left for school he was adjusting the valves.

I hurried home that afternoon, because I always went with him to Monroe on Friday nights.

We got in the truck—Daddy, Uncle Dub Coleman, and me. Uncle Dub was my mother's brother, and he always went to races with Daddy. We were just about to the race track when Daddy looked over at me and asked, "Got everything tight on that car back there? Nothing going to fall off, is it?"

I said, "Well, I think it's okay. I went over everything I could think of, and I laid in bed last night trying to think of something I could have overlooked. I don't think I missed anything."

He looked at me and asked, "Are you sure?"

When he said that, I mumbled under my breath. I knew right then he had found something, but I had no idea what.

I guess my chin dropped about an inch, and my pride probably fell down around my ankles.

I said, "I'm pretty sure, but let me think of everything again."

We got to the track and unloaded the car. I'm thinking, "Gosh, what has he found? What could I have missed?"

I waited until he was doing something, and I walked up beside him. I don't think I spoke very loud, but I said, "Daddy, I can't think of anything I left loose."

Whatever he was doing, he didn't look up, but I was pretty sure he was thinking something.

Daddy never raised the hood on a race car once he arrived at a track. That was one of the things he didn't do. When he got to the race track, that race car was ready to race.

I think that was his way of telling the competition, "I'm ready. How 'bout you?" I wanted to look under the hood so bad I didn't know what to do. I wanted to peek under there

> one more time and try to find something I had overlooked, but I wasn't going to raise the hood unless he said it was all right.
>
> Finally, it was about time for practice to begin. He came over to me and said, "Dale, I'll tell you what you better do. Maybe you better get two 9/16s wrenches and tighten those bolts on the radiator. I don't think they will hold for this race." I opened the hood and looked at the two bolts on each side of the radiator. Then I remembered that I ran the bolts up with my fingers and did not tighten them with wrenches.
>
> I wanted to crawl in a hole. For a minute I felt like the world's biggest failure. I was worried that I might not ever be able to install an engine and get it right.
>
> Then a good feeling came over me. I realized for the first time that Daddy had trusted me to fix his race car. It also showed me how much expertise he had.
>
> Now, take those bolts. By looking at them you would not be able to tell if they were loose or tight. What he noticed was that the lock washers behind the bolts were not mashed flat.
>
> It was a valuable lesson for me. It taught me to look beyond the obvious. After I tightened the bolts, closed the hood, and put up the tools, I asked Dad if that was all I left loose. He said it was all he could find, and that maybe nothing would fall off the car.
>
> He had a little twinkle in his eye, and he smiled.
>
> He may as well have given me a million dollars. That was his way of telling me everything was okay, and it let me know that he appreciated what I had done. Then he went out and won the race. That really made me feel good.[74]

Note the several places in which some quality of mindfulness appears in Earnhardt's story, even though he never called it precisely by that name. Even as a small child, he paid attention to his sweeping and absorbed himself so fully in it that he did it with excellence, understanding that he had not yet earned the right to touch the race cars but also understanding that his sweeping up was a lesson in the discipline that led his father to trust him. Later, he paid enough attention to the amount of clay on the radiator to know whether his father had won or finished second. That is an example of full awareness. Earnhardt was not so busy looking for the trophy that he overlooked more subtle evidence. He was so fully engaged in the moment that he noticed everything about it, including the amount of clay on the radiator.

When Earnhardt says his project with the car was "all I thought about in school," of course he is not bringing mindfulness to his studies, but for a kid who loved racing far more than he ever loved school, perhaps that is not too surprising. Nevertheless, the mindfulness was quick to return as soon as he got home and started work on the car. He said, "I thought about everything." Every action was undertaken with full, careful attention and total absorption. But notice particularly that he saved his worrying, his personal narrative that he might not be capable of the task, until after he had gone to bed. While working on the car, he seems to have shut off that unproductive and upsetting narrative in favor of careful action. Splitting his attention between worrying about his ability to install an engine and actually installing one would have made him less attentive, and even as a teen Earnhardt seems to have intuited that.

Earnhardt demonstrates paying attention to everything big and small about a moment, and he also demonstrates total absorption in the moment. It is his father, Ralph, who displays bare awareness. Actually, as Earnhardt himself notes, his father also "looked beyond the obvious," and to do so himself was a lesson from this experience that Earnhardt took deeply to heart. His father noted that the lock washers on the radiator were not flattened. But he did not jump to the conclusion that his son was not ready or able to install an engine. He did not scold the boy. He simply saw what needed to be done and asked his son to do it. He appears to have added no personal narrative to the event at all. That kind of calm noticing and doing is the essence of bare awareness. See what needs to be done and do it. Then see the next thing and do that. Then go out and win the race.

6

IMPERMANENCE

We want the real rose. We want the one that dies. We want it *because* it dies, *because* it's fleeting, *because* it fades. It's this very quality that makes it precious.[75]

Impermanence is simply the fact that nothing lasts forever. That nothing is permanent is obvious enough, but again, it is the kind of obvious truth with which the West seems uncomfortable. Not only do actors and actresses in Hollywood try to hold on to their youth with facelifts and Botox injections to mask aging, but ads for Rogaine and Viagra are everywhere. They tell us that "youth" can be had right up into one's sixties or seventies, an age that at the beginning of the last century was the end of the lifespan, or at least time to stop playing tennis and become a wise elder. Now that our elders are as youthful as anybody else (if not aggressively *more* so), where will we get our wisdom?

If you think about it, it is more than the impermanence of life itself that worries us. Of course, that is the big issue, but we resist impermanence in our relationships, possessions, and other areas of our lives as well. How many marital fights have begun, "You weren't like this when we were dating"? We hold on to images of our beloved that may have been formed years ago, out of early moments in the arc of their lives, when we were most taken by them. And all too often, rather than loving each developing stage of them as their lives have progressed, we want our beloved to stay the same, to have the same likes and dislikes or the same charm with which we had fallen in love. Similarly, we miss our children as gurgling babies and wish we had them back in our arms when the child is still right in front of us, slamming his door and turning up his unintelligible music.

We even long for permanence in our possessions. Most of us throw out possessions with a sense of perplexed betrayal. We tend to think, "How could that refrigerator have just *died* on me? Is that lamp really hopelessly broken? Maybe I should put it in the basement or attic for a while—you know, fix it later or figure out another use for it." Favorite clothes can be the hardest things to throw out. Who doesn't have a beloved sweatshirt that can no longer be worn in public but just can't be thrown out?

Nothing lasts forever. Everything in your house will one day be broken or decaying. You yourself will die. This is a teaching that the Buddha gave over and over. He told his first followers to meditate in cemeteries in order for them to begin to understand impermanence. For Hindu India, this command was a major cultural transgression since it was taboo for upper castes or ascetics to touch or even be near dead bodies. The Buddha insisted on this teaching, though, to break the taboo, to bring death back, front and center, in his students' minds.

The importance of this emphasis on death has often been misunderstood in the West and by people new to Buddhism. Evangelical Christians often criticize Buddhism as being death-obsessed, for instance, a characterization that shapes the initial impression of many other people too.

But far from being negative, the emphasis on impermanence is intended to affirm life by teaching us that this moment—every moment—is precious. Because everything will break or die eventually, treasure the moment *now*, and treasure it *fully*. People change. Love them now, for who they are now. And then tomorrow, love them for who they are then. If you love someone for who they are each moment, instead of comparing that moment to previous ones you liked better, then you automatically judge them less and appreciate their little quirks more. When you treat the whole world that way, the idea of judging and resisting the things you dislike and clinging to the things you like simply starts to fall away. You find that if you are able to love something for one moment, for only what it is in that moment, and then start over again in the next moment, you are capable of loving a whole lot more than you ever thought you could. This expansion of our ability to appreciate and love is the essence of the teaching of impermanence.

Thich Nhat Hanh is the Vietnamese Buddhist monk who was nominated for a Nobel Peace Prize by Dr. Martin Luther King Jr. He has a slightly different explanation of impermanence. He begins with the same idea that everything changes, but then goes on to show that impermanence is not only inevitable but necessary and beneficial:

> The teaching of impermanence should not be seen as negative or pessimistic. It is thanks to impermanence that everything is here. If a grain of corn, for example, were not impermanent, it could never become a corn plant, and we'd never have more corn to eat. If there were no impermanence, illness could never be cured. Instead of complaining that things are impermanent, we must welcome impermanence as a factor that makes life possible."[76]

Impermanence also sustains the path. If Buddhism is "quite simply...the great question of who or what we are, right here, now, at this very moment,"[77] then impermanence means that the great question is new again in each moment, as is our opportunity to practice. One might ask, "To practice what?" The answer can be as narrow as any single element on which you may wish to concentrate, such as practicing peace or practicing awareness. Alternately, the answer can be as large as "to practice life, to be aware without narrative and to be fully absorbed in each breath, each step, each word, and each action." Each moment is a microcosm in which we can establish an entire way of life. In the next moment, we begin again; and in the moment after that, we begin a third time. Buddhist practice consists of seeing these microcosms in each moment and stringing them together into minutes, hours, days, and lifetimes.

For me, impermanence was probably the first teaching that I truly understood. My parents divorced when I was small (something many children in America experience as their first lesson in impermanence), and my father reared me as a single parent from the time I was about ten. When I was nineteen, he died suddenly, essentially leaving me orphaned (although with a large and loving family on his side). By the time I was thirty, four college friends had died. Two of them never reached twenty-one, and the other two did not make it past thirty. My grandparents, who were particularly comforting to me after my father's death, also died during my twenties—within six months of each other—and another uncle not long after that. I am not sure when the lesson quite took hold of me, but while I procrastinate as much as the next person sometimes, for the most part I am always ready to get things moving, always ready for the next adventure. Stagnation feels like death to me, and while my relationship with my husband is reaching the twenty-year mark, I have scarcely lived in one town for more than five years in my entire life. Impermanence to me is sometimes an adventure and sometimes heartbreak, but it is something I *know*, bone-deep.

Moreover, impermanence has to me always been intimately intertwined with love. Besides being able to let go of judgments and appreciate each moment, understanding impermanence has a profound effect on every aspect of our relationships. The paradox of love is that it can only be lasting if it is also ever-changing. No one I love is the same person as they were when I first met them. Nor am I the same person I was when they first met me. Love grows, evolves, ebbs, flows, and transforms as it is transformed. In no way can love be permanent and unchanging. It changes from year to year and even from day to day, and our acceptance and embrace of that change is exactly the choice that allows love to last. When we resist loving each different stage of a person, then we find ourselves "growing apart," because love follows time's arrow, but we have tried to avoid doing the same. We have tried to make the love we felt twenty years ago serve the person of today—or tried to win today's race with last week's tires, to put it in NASCAR terms. To have lasting love is to be forever in a state of impermanence, and to willingly embrace that impermanence.

Again, I am not sure quite when I realized this connection between impermanence and love, but I don't think it is something that all my peers can say: I know what true love is. My grandparents had it, without a doubt. My grandmother died suddenly of a heart attack. At her viewing, my grandfather asked for some time alone with her. The funeral director was a decades-long friend of the family, and he stayed in the room, discreetly in the background, in case my grandfather collapsed or needed help. At the time, the funeral director told the rest of the family nothing, but when Granddaddy died six months later, the funeral director was one of the people who delivered eulogies. He told us that in that time alone, he had witnessed the meaning of true love. My grandfather had said to my grandmother, "Irene, I'm glad you went first—because I would *never* have wanted you to be the one to have to grieve. I would never have wanted you to feel what I'm feeling right now."

Beyond that shining example, I have figured out a few things about true love on my own, and most of them have to do with impermanence. It is easy to love someone when you're holding hands and walking down the beach together. You know that if he or she were to walk out the door at that moment, your world would fall apart. But in the middle of the worst fight you've ever had, could you say the same? If, at that moment, you could stop and think, "If this person walked out of my life right now, I would be miserable. We may be arguing about who does all the work around the house, but I would hate to lose him," then you know that your love is true. I have done that, and my anger and irritation vanished in a flash. I said, "You know what? We'll figure out who loads the damn dishwasher. It really doesn't matter. I only have one lifetime with you, and I don't want to waste a minute more of it fighting." What stopped the fight was that instant of thinking, "What if he were suddenly gone?" The realization of impermanence and the understanding of the preciousness of each moment have the power to dissolve anger completely.

That same realization can also free us from regret. Being aware of impermanence, I do think to the future about a time when my husband and I might no longer be together. What would be hardest for me would be regret. If I had to look back on times when I could have been more open or more honest, or more loving, it would be tremendously painful and hard to let go of the past. But when I embody my understanding of impermanence in my moment-to-moment behavior, then I make an effort to make each moment one I won't ever need to regret. So far, I regret practically nothing of our twenty years together. I have loved him deeply and truthfully, with as much of my heart as I had to give in each moment. If things were to end tomorrow, I wouldn't feel that I had wasted time, and without an understanding of impermanence, I don't know that I could say that.

Buddhists are not the only ones who realize impermanence deeply, but for most Westerners, they realize it too late. Consider this quote from film critic Joel Siegel: "Cancer changes your life, often for the better. You learn what's important, you learn to prioritize, and you learn not to waste your time. You tell people you love them. My friend Gilda Radner [who died of ovarian cancer in 1989 at age 42] used to say, 'If it wasn't for the downside, having cancer would be the best thing and everyone would want it.' That's true. If it wasn't for the downside." Most cancer survivors can tell you that they never lose this sense of time being short and precious. They never lose the wisdom of prioritizing and not wasting time, and they never lose the wisdom of telling people they love them. But it can be late in life before that lesson is learned, and for those who do not survive, it comes at the very end. I consider myself extremely lucky to have realized it much younger than most people. Whether it was Buddhism that taught me impermanence, or whether the impermanence in my own life's events inclined me toward Buddhism as a path, I have been able to use the fact of impermanence as a way to embrace life in the present moment.

NASCAR drivers understand impermanence in the most profound ways. The first and most obvious way they understand it is in the sport's inherent risk of death. Drivers are careful about keeping their wills up to date, because they know that almost any weekend could be their last. Even "safe" tracks have caused fatalities. The two shortest tracks on the circuit are Bristol and Martinsville, neither considered particularly dangerous. But both are nestled into the often-foggy Blue Ridge Mountains, and plane crashes on the way to each track have claimed the lives of over a dozen people in the sport.

NASCAR drivers also understand impermanence in more subtle ways. First, they understand it as letting go of events after they are over. There are thirty-six races in each year, for the most part in consecutive weeks. There is no time to hold on to one race or nurse a grudge from it. (Grudges do occur between drivers and teams, but they are relatively infrequent and generally short-lived, and most drivers say the grudges are far more media hype than reality.) As soon as a driver has parked the race car on Sunday afternoon, he goes home and by Monday afternoon is planning for the next race, thinking about which car to use in that event and how to set it up. In a career, there will be hundreds, even thousands of races, and what is past simply has to be past, both good and bad. Winning is a great feeling, but come Monday afternoon the driver needs to stop patting himself on the back and get ready to face another track and another challenge. And losing is an awful feeling, but only if the driver hangs on to it does the team spiral into self-doubt.

Letting even the worst finishes go and moving forward is essential. In 2002, Tony Stewart finished dead last in the Daytona 500, but by season's end he was the NASCAR Cup champion because he and his team were able to shake off the disappointment and bounce back. So drivers understand impermanence through the practice of being resilient. Winning one week will not sustain a driver for the whole season, but losing one week won't destroy him for the whole season either. Everything is temporary—both good and bad—the Buddhist believes; and because nothing lasts, a Buddhist simply takes whatever happens, lets it go, and keeps moving on.

Even in the course of a single race, a driver must deal with impermanence. A flat tire can put a team a lap down, and when that happens, the crew chief tells his driver, "Shake it off. Shake it off, and keep digging." It is not at all uncommon for the winning team to have been a lap down at one point in the day, and in victory lane the driver will allude to the problem and say, "Yeah, we got down a little bit early on, but didn't let that take our focus away. We just kept after it and wound up winning." Using their mental discipline to let the past fall *immediately* into the past, drivers shrug off obstacles, remain focused on the goal, and succeed because they did not get bogged down clinging to the past. Race fans may not always see the mental discipline or the philosophy hidden in it, but there is a lesson for everyone's life in that deceptively simple phrase, "Shake it off, and keep digging," and a fine Buddhist teaching to boot.

Exemplifying this practice of letting things go, Dale Earnhardt said, "What happened last week just happened last week. It is over and done with. That is the way this team treats it. We race one week and go on to the next race."[78] He was serious about that. Once, he had had a serious altercation with another driver. Alluding to the on-track confrontation, a reporter asked him, "What about last week?" Earnhardt looked genuinely blank for a moment and replied, "What about it?" He had completely forgotten the incident, and only remembered when the reporter asked about the other driver by name. True to his philosophy, Earnhardt said that the whole thing was over as far as he was concerned.

Drivers also understand impermanence in another sense, knowing what they cannot control. Humans cannot control the passage of time or the fact that things and people change whether we want them to or not. Struggling against this perfectly obvious fact is a source of suffering for many people, although they never realize the true cause of their suffering. "If only things could be different" is one of the most useless phrases ever uttered. Indeed, we have the power to change some things, and we are either acting to bring about a change or we are not. If we are, then we are doing all we can. If we are not, then we are doing nothing, and why would we expect change to appear as the result of nothing? Some things, we do not have the power to change. In those cases, struggling will only cause suffering. As the Dalai Lama cheerfully observes, "If there is a solution for a problem, no point in being overwhelmed and worrying; and if there is no solution for a problem, no point in being overwhelmed and worrying about it!"[79] Christian theologian Reinhold Neibuhr's beautiful Serenity Prayer ("Lord, grant me the serenity to accept the things I cannot change, the courage to change the things I can, and the wisdom to know the difference") comes from exactly the same understanding as this facet of impermanence. We should recognize those circumstances that we cannot change and accept them, realizing that they are impermanent.

For former crew chief and driver Kirk Shelmerdine, personal control relates to circumstances as a surfer relates to the ocean. He says, "Success is like surfing. You're doing what you can to stay on the board, but you really aren't in control of anything. And the more you think you're in control, the more you're going to wipe out. You have to realize that all you can do is hang on as best you can. You don't have any control over anything else."[80] Relinquishing our *illusion* of control is similar to the notion of emptiness in chapter 2. We do our actions as nearly perfectly and mindfully as we can, but that is all we can do. We cannot necessarily control the outcome. NASCAR drivers may prepare the car perfectly, condition their body and mind, practice extensively, and still finish last because a two-dollar bolt broke or because they had nowhere to go on the track when another driver blew a tire and spun into them. Nevertheless, if they do not do their actions with all their hearts and all the excellence they have in them, then they are never creating the conditions for winning either.

Of course, understanding what you don't control is helpful for everyday life as well as for more esoteric pursuits like driving a race car or meditating. People get caught up in thinking, "I have to win" or "This has to work out." When they are clinging that tightly to one result, they get tunnel vision and fail to see how any other outcome could be good for them. Thus, only if their very specific desire is very specifically satisfied are they happy; otherwise, they feel defeated and miserable. But the fact is, there may be any number of positive outcomes.

In your own efforts, similar or not, you might not get the outcome you wanted, but you may learn something about yourself, or something about another person, or you may learn a practice that will help you down the road, or you might get a positive result you hadn't foreseen. But if you are too busy lamenting that you didn't get the one outcome you wanted, you won't see any of these things as good. In fact, you won't really see them at all because you'll be too blinded by regret. So offer your very best effort, but let the result be whatever it is—and then move beyond it. Take a result you did not want and examine it to see whether it might not work out just as well or even better; or examine the result for how it might help you to grow and expand your definition of outcomes you can accept. My husband, in search of a particular type of headlight that he knew only by sight, bought about half a dozen sets of headlights that all turned out to be wrong. Installing the last pair, he stepped back and said, "No, these aren't exactly it either." Then he paused, shrugged, and said, "But, hey, I've got a lifetime supply of headlights." That immediate reframing allowed him to chuckle at the whole enterprise and see the good in what some people might have seen as a setback. Some people have the natural ability to reframe negative events in this manner (even extremely negative events—see above how Gilda Radner reframed cancer as a way to become a more loving person, although it clearly wasn't the outcome that she had wanted for her life). But the skill can be practiced and learned so that even a person who has thought of himself or herself as a pessimist or who sees such events as defeats can learn to reframe them. Practicing impermanence and accepting what we cannot control helps us achieve this easy, humorous peace with outcomes other than the one we had in mind.

Lastly, rather than seeing the glass as half-empty or half-full, one who knows impermanence sees it, with all the good humor one might expect, as "already broken." Why do we curse when we drop a glass? Because we don't understand impermanence. A lama laughingly tells Buddhist psychotherapist Mark Epstein, "You see this goblet? For me, this glass is already broken. I enjoy it; I drink out of it. It holds my water admirably, sometimes even reflecting the sun in beautiful patterns. If I should tap it, it has a lovely ring to it. But when I put this glass on a shelf and the wind knocks it over or my elbow brushes it off the table and it falls to the ground and shatters, I say, 'Of course,' [because] when I understand that this glass is already broken, every moment with it is precious."[81] This open-hearted, relaxed perspective is what many non-practitioners misunderstand about Buddhism. It may seem overly focused on death or decay or impermanence, but that is because, followed completely through to its logical conclusion, impermanence actually brings us to great joy. When the glass is already broken, when we can imagine the people we love disappearing tomorrow, then we pause for a moment to enjoy the sun's patterns on the glass or the simple presence of the person we love. We drop our habitual preoccupations and love people fiercely, completely. We live this moment, and all our moments, with gratitude and expansiveness, as richly as we can.

7

PATIENCE, ENDURANCE (KSHANTI)

> He had all kinds of talent but he did not have the heart to lose. Some may think that is a good thing. But if you play sports, you better be able to handle loss. Life is just the same.[82]

By now, most Americans with even a passing interest in NASCAR know the story of Dale Earnhardt's tragedies, triumph, and final, mortal, tragedy at Daytona. He won more events there than any other driver in history, but only once was he able to win the "Great American Race"—the Daytona 500. In the twenty years that he tried to win and failed before finally breaking through in 1998, he had lost the race in just about every way imaginable. He notched a record five second-place finishes, leading him to quip ruefully that he was five-time champion of the "Daytona 499." He ran out of gas, got passed, ran over parts that fell off other cars, blew tires, and once even hit a seagull on the backstretch. Destiny and even nature itself seemed against him ever winning the crown jewel of stock-car racing. So Earnhardt's experiences at Daytona are a fitting place to begin a chapter on endurance and patience.

In the Mahayana sect of Buddhism, practitioners are taught to embody in their thought, speech, and behavior six *paramitas*, or virtues. Taken from the Lotus Sutra, these virtues are

—*Dana* (generosity)
—*Sila* (ethics, discipline, morality)
—*Kshanti* (patience, endurance, forbearance)
—*Viriya* (diligence, determined effort—from which we get the word "virile")
—*Dhyana* (one-pointed concentration, contemplation)
—*Prajna* (wisdom, insight)

The subject of this chapter is *kshanti.* In both racing and spiritual terms, it means facing setbacks or adversity with patience and using them to grow stronger and wiser. The best example of *kshanti* I can think of is the wheel on the wall at Richard Childress Racing.

At RCR, Earnhardt's home shop, there is a battered wheel, the blown-out tire still on it, mounted on a wooden plaque and hanging on the wall with a brass plate beneath it recording the date, February 18, 1990, and the time and place, turn 4, last lap, Daytona 500 (unbeknownst to anyone, the plaque on the wall was also silently prophesying the date, time, and place of Earnhardt's death exactly eleven years later—February 18, turn 4, last lap, Daytona 500). On the last turn of the last lap in the 1990 Daytona 500, Earnhardt was leading. In fact, he led 155 of the race's 200 laps. But in the last turn, with the checkered flag in sight, he ran over a sharp fragment of bell housing that had broken off another car. His tire blew out, and while he struggled to keep from wrecking, virtually unknown driver Derrike Cope swept around him for the win.

Earnhardt's car had been so strong the week leading up to the race that most reporters and other teams were convinced that he would win. The anticipation of a victory was so strong that, afterward, Earnhardt told reporters, "This was the biggest buildup and the biggest letdown I've ever had in racing. There's nothing you can do about it, either. You've just got to take it and go on,"[83] a sentiment his car owner Richard Childress echoed, calling the outcome a heartbreaker.

That flattened right front tire symbolized one of the team's lowest moments, its greatest defeat. Yet it wound up mounted on the wall at the race shop, almost as though in a place of honor, certainly in a place where team members could see it every day. It was put there to remind the team that success can be fleeting and that one should always stay humble because there's no telling what's around the next turn. And that, to me, is the heart of a champion—to be able to look his or her greatest defeat in the face every day, without flinching, and turn it into a positive. Very few people, I think, would willingly have a reminder of their deepest disappointment, their heartbreak, their biggest failure placed in front of them every day. But a champion is able to do that—*wants* to do it even, because they have mastered the *paramita* of patience and endurance. It took courage for everyone on the team to face that wheel every day, and that courage bound them together and made them a stronger, better team.

Both NASCAR and Buddhism focus extensively on enduring and overcoming disappointment: NASCAR because out of forty-three teams, only one will win each weekend, and the other forty-two are disappointed; and Buddhism because the First Noble Truth is about the subtle sense of disappointment and unease that haunts daily life. Both may seem to start from a negative or depressing premise, but both also ultimately promise joy. Any race-car driver will say that years of struggle and heartbreak vanish the moment he pulls into victory lane for the first time, and any Buddhist will tell you that when one accepts the reality of *dukkha*, one enjoys the sweet moments with more gratitude and more intensity, and the joy one gets from those moments will sustain one in future times of struggle.

The most common reaction to talking about acceptance of problems and patience in the face of adversity is a turning away, a cry that "no one wants problems!" Many people will say that if you "accept" problems, then that must mean you passively sit back and do nothing to improve your lot, merely allowing the problems to continue and worsen in the name of acceptance. As Earnhardt's wheel on the wall shows, accepting a problem does not mean allowing it to continue or repeat. He and the team displayed the wheel in order to make them better, as a spur to remind them that the greatest wins would come only to those who could rise above the greatest heartbreaks. Accepting the reality of problems does not mean allowing them to rule your life; rather, accepting their reality becomes the first step toward calmly solving them, while living in denial or seething with resentment *does* let problems fester.

Zen teacher Charlotte Joko Beck speaks of how often her students start out by reacting with anger and irritation at setbacks. She calls this response the moment of "that's not what I want!" and says it is exactly this response that we must unpack the meaning of and consider carefully. Who is the "I" doing the wanting? Usually, it is mostly ego, the pride-seeking part of us, or id, the pleasure-seeking part, so it is our inflated sense of self that is being pricked or our habitual indolence and self-indulgence being challenged. What is this "wanting"? Why is our wanting more important than another person's? Why does anger so often seem the natural response to failing to get what we want? Where does this aggression in defending our pride and our comfort come from? Does it come from knowing deep down that we really need neither our usual level of pride nor of comfort, and a sense of guilt at desiring them so nakedly, thus resulting in defensiveness and anger?

Beck teaches *kshanti* by using this moment of anger as a "gateway" to the Zen practice of self-inquiry. She says,

> The more we're aware of our expectations, the more we see that our urge is to manipulate life rather than live it just as it is. Students whose practice is maturing aren't angry as often because they see their expectations, their desires, before they produce anger. But if the stage of anger is reached, it is practice. Our signal to practice, our "red light," is at the point of upset, the disappointment, [the] "it's not the way I want it!" Some expectation has not been fulfilled and we sense the irritability, frustration, the desire to have it otherwise. "I want" has been frustrated. This very point when "I want" has been frustrated is the "gateless gate"—because the only way to transform "I want" into "I am" is to experience one's disappointment, one's frustration [and move beyond it].[84]

Drivers learn to shrug off defeats and bad breaks the same way. Their "I want" gets frustrated on a weekly basis, but they learn, as Earnhardt did, that "there's nothing you can do about it. You just have to take it and go on." All athletes seem to understand this natural outcome of sports, and they adjust to take setbacks philosophically rather than personally in a way that many other people do not. No matter what their sport, athletes learn to do the mental work of their game, and they develop a sense of discipline that serves them in life as well as on the field of play. The thousands of pro and semi-pro athletes around the nation are not particularly exalted specimens of humanity, any more so than the millions of practicing Buddhists who follow the same discipline of patience and endurance. Rather, this skill can be learned by anyone who wants to make the effort to learn it. If setbacks take the wind out of your sails, then you might learn *kshanti* from Buddhism, or you might learn to put that wheel right up on the wall and look at it like Earnhardt did, or you might learn from any athlete who tells a reporter, "Yep, that was a hard loss to take, but we'll get 'em next week." Whatever "gateless gate" through which you enter, the destination—patience and endurance—is the same.

Buddhist writer John Snelling, author of *The Buddhist Handbook: A Complete Guide to Buddhist Schools, Teaching, Practice, and History*, puts the Second Noble Truth, grasping or clinging, in the context of patience when he says, "Good things do come to us in the course of events and should be accepted and enjoyed while they last, but we tend to want *only* the good and, resisting all else, pursue it exclusively and cling to it desperately if we do get it."[85] This approach leads to suffering through the emotional violence of resisting, fighting, struggling, pursuing, clinging, and fear of losing. From this outlook comes our violence against one another, as we all try to "look out for number one," and from this outlook comes the spiritual exhaustion and violence of denying the reality of life, which is that we get good and bad mixed together, whether we want it that way or not.

So many people seem to take the difficult times in their lives as a personal affront and something to be escaped as quickly as possible. When one does not resist the problem, one instead asks, "What can I learn from what's happening to me now?" It might seem surprising, but once the fear and resistance are swept away, problems can become very interesting things, even productive challenges, as one gleans knowledge about oneself and learns about one's own resilience and ingenuity. Pema Chödrön, a beloved Buddhist nun and prolific author, writes,

> Generally speaking, we regard discomfort in any form as bad news. But for practitioners or spiritual warriors—people who have a certain hunger to know what is true—feelings like disappointment, embarrassment, irritation, resentment, anger,

> jealousy, and fear, instead of being bad news, are actually very clear moments that teach us where it is that we're holding back.... They're like messengers that show us, with terrifying clarity, exactly where we're stuck. This very moment is the perfect teacher, and, lucky for us, it's with us wherever we are.[86]

Her notion of being "stuck" is an elegantly simple way of explaining practice. The goal is for all of life's events to flow like a river, unimpeded, through us, as we maintain our equanimity and respond with the necessary actions. The moments when we feel the flow stop or hit a block are the moments when we are resisting life as it is, and those are the moments when Buddhists stop and say, "This is something I need to work on." And her notion of "spiritual warriors" is important as well—these are people who take life's setbacks, face them honestly, and use them to become stronger. While they savor life's little triumphs, they fully accept the impermanence of that moment of pleasure. Spiritual warriors neither avoid problems nor cling to pleasure. They simply accept whatever arises in the moment before them and respond from their highest ideals. Buddhists do not believe that such spiritual warriors are specially marked out or chosen for this kind of practice. On the contrary, they believe that it is completely accessible to anyone who chooses it. Anyone who joins the battle to see discomfort as a teacher is a warrior, and those who do not join this battle are trapped in the *samsaric* dream world of endlessly spiraling pleasure and pain, unable to say with the Buddha, "I am awake."

Chödrön also writes that for many years she kept a sign on her wall that read, "Only to the extent that we expose ourselves over and over to annihilation can that which is indestructible be found in us."[87] I love this quote—it inspires me to take chances and fearlessly to try new experiences. For Buddhists, the annihilation is that of ego or self, but this concept of finding the indestructible is an explanation of why everyone, to one degree or another, is a thrill seeker, why we gamble and bungee jump and watch scary movies. These activities are small, safely contained ways to risk annihilation, and in a small, safely contained way, they show us glimpses of the indestructible in us, the intense, joyous engagement with the moment that comes when we "survive" the all-in bet or the jump or the movie. True adventurers take greater risks, like driving race cars, and in so doing they find greater understanding of the indestructible part of their spirit. Consequently, athletes and adventurers are daring and confident and charismatic. The ones who have repeatedly taken great risks are the most confident and charismatic of all, and they are also the ones who seem most comfortable in their skins. They are "the greats" of any sport, and from Jordan to Negreanu to Tiger Woods to Earnhardt, they all seem to share this trait of having found that which is indestructible in themselves.

Buddhist teachers often have the same personality. The greatest risk of all is faced by those persons at the end of life, and in the fight against terminal illnesses such as cancer, for example, we see seemingly ordinary people rise to this level of wisdom and grace. This is why the Buddha told his followers to meditate on death—so that they would face the ultimate annihilation over and over until they had achieved a similar awareness of their indestructible spirit. Had the Buddha been alive in modern America, he might have been an inspirational, intellectual, life-changing type of coach like Vince Lombardi or Joe Torre—or perhaps the Buddha would have been Phil Jackson, sometimes called "the Zen Master" or "the basketball Buddha" for his calm demeanor and his urging that players meditate together.

Western artists and philosophers have also understood the nature of *kshanti*, or patience. On this topic, Leonardo da Vinci wrote, "Patience serves as a protection against wrongs as clothes do against cold, for if you put on more clothes as the cold increases, it will have no power to hurt you. So in like manner you must grow in patience when you meet with great wrongs, and they will be powerless to vex you."[88] Trappist monk Thomas Merton takes a similar tack to Pema Chödrön's response to realizing where we are "stuck." According to Merton, "Prayer and love are learned in the very hour when prayer becomes impossible and the heart has turned to stone."[89] Ascetics, athletes, philosophers, Buddhists—essentially, all those who undertake a search for higher consciousness—realize that instead of something to be avoided, difficulties and pain are exactly the moments that can teach us the most; in fact, the "spiritual warrior" should welcome them when they arise. Earnhardt might not have articulated this sustained confrontation with difficulty and pain in the same way, even as his story about mindfulness is articulated in the language of red clay on radiators and lock washers mashed flat rather than the language of the Lotus Sutra and *paramitas.* But the wheel on the wall tells us he knew the same truth about patience and endurance—*kshanti*—that any other spiritual warrior knows.

The ultimate virtue of patience is that it helps us avoid becoming overwhelmed. It also reminds us of the moment-to-moment nature of Buddhist practice. Joseph Goldstein says, "Often we are discouraged by the enormity of a task or the length of a journey.... We lose faith in ourselves. Patience reminds us that what is in front of us is *just this moment, just this step, just this breath*"[90] [italics mine].

Drivers take the same approach. They cope with each issue as it arises, dealing with just this turn, just this pass, just this lap. They begin their careers one step at a time, with the patience to start small. Many would-be drivers take any job they can get in a race shop, simply to put their faces in front of the right people and to be in place and ready should an opportunity ever open up. For instance, Bobby Labonte took a job sweeping up the shop at Joe Gibbs Racing. He didn't cling to the idea of "they have to hire me to drive," but he held on to that dream while agreeing to be the shop janitor. He performed his job mindfully and with as much dedication and excellence as possible so that, when higher positions became available, the Gibbs team trusted his dedication. It took patience, but eventually he became their driver, a millionaire, with fans and a team jet and media exposure. Had he been attached to an ego-driven image of himself as a driver all along, he probably would not have deigned to take the job sweeping up. Because he understood, correctly, that sweeping up was a step on the path, and because he approached each step with the same devotion to excellence that he planned to show as a driver, by the time he was offered the driving job, Joe Gibbs knew that Bobby was the kind of driver he wanted.

Ernie Irvan took a similar path, starting out welding seats at the Charlotte, North Carolina, track and unloading moving vans for people involved in racing, finally becoming a winning top-level driver by being patient and approaching even small tasks with dedication. In so doing, he earned the notice of people in the sport who helped him move up. Former racing journalist Ronda Rich said, "I thought you just barreled out of the starting gate with anything you did and went straight for the top. But as I watched those who were destined for stardom chip through smaller goals to large ones, I realized that the true path to great success is a journey of failures and small successes strung together."[91] From taking each small step to overcoming setbacks, patience is key. Zen Buddhists practice in the same way—by doing every task, no matter how small it may seem, with absorption and awareness. As a result, when enlightenment comes, they are already trained to approach it with awareness and not to miss it.

"Keep digging" is a common saying in NASCAR. It means don't give up, have patience and endurance, have fortitude, be resilient. Practice *kshanti.* Everyone in NASCAR has a story about someone who keeps digging and eventually finds what they need. Darrell Waltrip says of his brother Michael's struggles to become a driver, "He never yielded, just kept right on digging. When somebody slammed the door, he went and found another one [to] open."[92] Dale Earnhardt Jr. says of the intense pressure he faced, "I use it to my advantage. That's the only way this deal's going to work—if everything that could be a negative gets made into a positive."[93] The general media may treat NASCAR drivers as none-too-bright country boys, but from rookie to veteran, they have a considerable amount of wisdom to offer anyone who pays attention. The insights of Waltrip and Earnhardt Jr. apply not only to themselves and other NASCAR drivers, but also to ordinary folks encountering everyday problems.

Ronda Rich spent several years working in the racing world. She, too, kept an ear tuned to the wisdom that drivers had to offer, and she shares it in her memoir *My Life in the Pits.* She formed a particularly close friendship with the late Alan Kulwicki. Kulwicki was the underdog of underdogs, a smart but serious and reserved Yankee in a sport full of boisterous southerners. He was an owner-driver at a time when that business model was dying out because of the impossibility of being CEO and driver at the same time. And he was driving for his own single-car team just when it was becoming obvious that multi-car teams had all but insurmountable competitive advantages. Some of the time he drove without sponsorship, a financially crippling proposition. Other drivers didn't always know quite what to make of Kulwicki, who could be standoffish at times, so he had few close friends in racing. His dogged determination made him, against all odds, the 1992 NASCAR champion. But he only got to enjoy the fruits of his labor for about six months. In April 1993, on his way to a race in Bristol, Tennessee, his plane crashed into a mountainside in bad weather, killing Kulwicki and everyone aboard. Alan Kulwicki was deeply thoughtful and philosophical, and Rich says she learned a great deal from being his friend.

Kulwicki (like me) loved quotes and used them as reminders of the life he wanted to lead. Two lines he repeated often were, "Obstacles are what you see when you take your eyes off the goal," attributed to Henry Ford, and, "Racing is like life. If you get up one more time than you fall, you'll make it through."[94] Rich says of him, "[Alan] analyzed adversity and setbacks and then set about to solve them. He didn't take them as a sign that his dream was no more than pie in the sky. As he encountered difficulties, he simply devised ways to dispose of them."[95]

But Rich learned the most about managing disappointment from Bobby Allison, a racing legend. His story, familiar to all race fans, is almost unbearably sad. In 1988, he and his son Davey finished first and second in the Daytona 500 and celebrated together in an emotional victory lane. However, later that year, Bobby was nearly killed at Pocono in a wreck that ended his racing career. He spent several days in a coma, and brain damage robbed him of many memories, including the one of his father-son finish with Davey. In 1992, his son Clifford died in a racing accident. Less than a year later, Davey, his only surviving son, was killed in a helicopter crash. Robbed of his career, his children, and even his memories, Allison has suffered more than anyone ought to. It took time, but he has survived and earned a measure of peace, telling Rich, "If I asked God why he let bad things happen to me, I'd also have to question why He gave me so many good things. If I'm not willing to question the good in life, I certainly can't question the bad."[96] From a heart that was broken too many times to count, that is patience and forbearance in action.

"In Zen practice," says teacher Taizan Maezumi Roshi, "we speak of three prerequisites for practice: great faith, great doubt, and great determination."[97] (There is another wonderful, related adage: "Great doubt, great enlightenment. Little doubt, little enlightenment. No doubt, no enlightenment.") Athletes seem to me to be like this as well. They have great faith in their skills. Perhaps paradoxically, they can also have great doubt—the industry of sports psychology exists in large part to work with this doubt, to keep it from turning into a persistent slump, or to help athletes maintain the mindset that helps them overcome difficulties. They also have great determination to see their efforts through, in the face of injury, doubt, setback, years of dues-paying, pain, and even heartbreak. It takes great faith, great doubt, and great determination to make a race-car driver or a Buddhist—and as the quote that opens this chapter observes, "Life is just the same."

8

DISCIPLINE, ENERGY, EFFORT (VIRIYA)

> No one wants to quit when he's losing. And no one wants to quit when he's winning.
>
> —Richard Petty[98]

Discipline and effort are pretty self-explanatory. Both Buddhism and NASCAR exemplify a firm belief in the virtue of effort. Both make explicit as teachings the idea that our success depends primarily on our own efforts and our own dedication to a goal.

It occurs to me that many Americans seem to find "discipline" an unpleasant word, evoking rigid, abusive punishment or the neurotic self-control of an anorexic. I do not mean "discipline" in that sense at all. Rather, for me (as a Buddhist), "discipline" is simply the will to carry out what is needed. It takes discipline to commit to a deadline and meet it, discipline to write a paper for a college class rather than blowing it off, and discipline to pay the bills even if that means not being able to go out to dinner with friends. Although it may force us to "choose the difficult" from time to time, there is nothing neurotic or abusive about this type of discipline; rather, it is a mindset we need in order to be successful in life. Athletes mean the same thing when they talk about discipline, and it is clear that they understand it as a virtue to be cultivated rather than as some kind of self-imposed punishment.

The beginning of discipline is practice, the art of learning. Zen teacher Taizan Maezumi Roshi considers the method, pace, and purpose of learning discipline:

> Raising *samadhi* [absorbed awareness] power is always gradual; no one can do it overnight. I think this is true for any kind of practice. You do the same thing over and over, just practicing the most basic thing. When I was a kid, I practiced Japanese archery. You draw the bow over and over in order to master the form. You need to learn how to pull, how much to pull, how to face the target, how to open the legs, where to hit.... In art, in sports, in music, in anything, we practice basic things over and over. When we do this kind of practice we become stronger, both mentally and physically.[99]

Similarly, a crew chief will remind a young driver, "Just drive your race. Just hit your marks." He does not comment on what other drivers are doing or how his driver compares to the leaders; if his driver is leading and is a nervous youngster, he won't tell the kid whether anyone is catching up to him. Instead, he calmly tells the driver to focus on what he is doing in each moment, to do it with excellence, and to practice the discipline that years of driving in lower divisions have taught him: enter each turn at the right moment, pull out of each turn smoothly, transition to the next turn cleanly. Over and over again, he tells the driver to simply practice the same basic skill until he has it, and in the process he will find a stronger, stiller mind and body. Several young drivers have been talked to victory lane in exactly this way, by being reminded over the last nerve-wracking laps to clear their minds and return to their basic discipline, because if they are turning laps cleanly and perfectly each time, no one will catch up to them. In the same way, Buddhist meditators return to the breath, practicing the basic discipline of awareness. Practicing these basic skills over and over gives them a twofold impact: first, the skills are something calming and familiar to which we can return in times of stress; second, they give us a solid, reliable foundation on which to build greater skills.

Effort is a fairly simple thing, and so is meditation. But as one Buddhist teacher observes, "Simple things are often hard to fully realize, so people need all kinds of aids and supports."[100] We need supports and aids, as well as mental tricks and a little internal negotiating with ourselves, because the discipline, energy, and effort that comprise the Buddhist concept of *viriya* have an opposite force—the phenomenon of *resistance.*

We all experience resistance. It frames itself as "I don't like," "I don't want," "this is no fun," "this is boring," "I don't feel like," "I'm not up to it right now." Basically, we are resisting any time we find ourselves reacting to something we know is good for us or something we know we really ought to do with some form of "no." Buddhist thinkers and writers, from the Buddha to present-day teachers throughout America, have devoted a great deal of discussion to resistance, because when we examine our thoughts and feelings routinely, it becomes clear that most of us are full of resistance. We resist life, as Charlotte Joko Beck says, preferring to manipulate it rather than welcoming it as it is. Pema Chödrön's description of being "stuck" is the same thing, and both counsel that we should aim to accept life in all its "suchness," however it comes to us. As Chödrön says, we should even—especially—accept the unpleasant moments, because they show us our resistance so clearly.

The technique for overcoming resistance is to query it closely. When you feel resistance, ask yourself *why* you are feeling it and what you might do to feel differently about it—whether or not the resistance is just that old monkey mind chattering away, the ego-consciousness standing apart from us. Ask yourself what it might feel like if you were utterly absorbed in whatever it is you are resisting, even if it is unpleasant. What would it feel like really to *know* this experience deeply, to explore its every nook and cranny, to sit with it as it ebbs and flows? For one thing, if it ever reappeared (and most things we resist *do* reappear), you would be more prepared to deal with it.

The way that absorption is the antidote for resistance is another example of how each step of Buddhism tends to underlie and support every other step, so that ideas and teachings tend to loop around and refer to each other. Buddhism is like a net, with each knot reaching out to other knots in all directions, no center and no linear sequence, but all touching one another. To say it more concretely, so far we have touched upon the "knots" of the Eightfold Path, and "knots" like the *paramitas* of effort, concentration, discipline, and patience. The net between the knots is the way that each teaching reinforces the others. To reiterate the example I gave in chapter 2, if we practice Right Speech, the goal is to have our speech be succinct and truthful, only what is needed at the moment it is needed. If we practice Right Mindfulness, we are trained to watch our thoughts, words, and actions. Thus, watching our words via Right Mindfulness supports and reinforces our practice of Right Speech.

Similarly, resistance is related to the difficulty in shutting off that observer mentality. We resist because a running commentary in our minds says, "This is no fun. I don't want to do this." That voice is only present because we are not fully absorbed in the task, because we have leftover ego with its unnecessary and intrusive commentary. This is not to say that we should not think about anything, that our minds should be empty when we are working. In a state of creative flow, a writer's running commentary is *about* the writing, sparking new ideas as the writer works. For an athlete in flow, the mental chatter may seem quieted, but at exactly the right moment, a thought appears about the next move. It is the running commentary that distracts us from flow that we aim to quell. Flow in sports (or in life) is related to quelling our resistance. To achieve flow we must exert effort, and the key obstacle to exerting effort is resistance. The good news is that the solutions are exactly the same: the *paramitas* of mindfulness, ethical behavior, effort, and so on untangle the snare of resistance, helping us to master absorption in each task, giving us the mindfulness that inspires us to careful effort. Right Action and Right Concentration support and are supported by *viriya*, or energy and effort, so that as soon as we call upon any one element of Buddhism to help us overcome resistance, the entire interwoven net is suddenly at our fingertips.

Resistance, then, is a chattering, disagreeing mind and a dissatisfied heart. Despite resistance, our goal is clarity of mind and stillness of heart. From a clear mind and still heart, our actions are simple, direct, and effective. Similarly, in a NASCAR race, when a driver needs to drive ten clean, mistake-free fast laps to get to victory, he needs to stop thinking about his opponents' lap times, what will happen if he slips up, how far it is to the checkered flag, how much money the victory will mean, or anything else. He needs most of all to return to his basic discipline and focus on each turn, each lap. Only what we can do in this breath, this moment, constitutes our true nature.

Initially, we might wonder how accepting life as it is and abolishing resistance are related to the intense, goal-driven effort necessary to be a race-car driver or a monk seeking enlightenment. There is no real conflict. On the contrary, clearing our minds of moment-to-moment resistance and quibbles with life leaves more room for us to hold a clear, vivid image of our ultimate goal, and when our hearts are still and our actions come out of that stillness, we can make them more goal-directed and effective, less scattered and reactive. The difference is between being reactive and proactive. To be proactive, we must not react to every little thing. We need to weed out all the small, unnecessary reactions. When we clear them away, we will have an open field ready for our proactive work on our goals. Likewise, a crew chief tells a driver when he is complaining about his competitors, "You can't drive everybody else's car for them. Just drive your own car." There is a fine line between being aware of everything and also knowing how much of that to let go; the difference is between what you can *know*, which is a great deal in any given moment, and what you can *do*, which is one perfect thing.

So effort, like so many other things, rests in the mind, and our mindset is crucial to our ultimate success. Stephen Batchelor recounts an anecdote of a Tibetan lama who was asked by a superstitious follower, "What will my future hold?" "It's very easy to find that out," the lama replied. "Just look into your present state of mind, and there you will see your future."[101]

Western philosophers have reached the same conclusions about undertaking effort. A much-quoted couplet from Goethe reads in full, "Whatever you can do, or dream you can, begin it / Boldness has genius, power, and magic in it."[102] Echoing that notion, Henry David Thoreau wrote, "Though I do not believe that a plant will spring up where no seed has been, I have great faith in a seed. Convince me that you have a seed there, and I am prepared to expect wonders."[103] And the Dalai Lama said cheerfully,

> Within a short time-span, it is impossible to change all our concepts or the entire attitude of our mind. It needs constant application. Speaking from my own small experience, from the age of about sixteen or seventeen, I began to make

> some serious effort to change and improve my outlook. Now at fifty-five, some thirty-nine years have gone by, several decades have passed, yet still the result is not satisfactory! We do have to struggle, and to work hard—and that is the reality.[104]

Although there might be different opinions about the satisfactoriness of the Dalai Lama's spiritual progress, the fact remains that both personal growth and worldly success take effort. There are schools of Buddhism that hold that we are already inherently enlightened. The metaphor they use is that of a buried jewel. We all have the perfection of buddhanature inside. The difference is whether or not we will make the effort to clear away the dirt covering that jewel. If we never make the effort, the jewel will never be seen. If we make some effort, some glimmers may appear, but only if we really carefully sweep away all the dirt (bad habits, clinging, selfish motivations, etc.) will the jewel fully shine for everyone to see and fully enrich our lives. Even if you and I are already Buddhas, effort makes all the difference in whether or not we live as Buddhas.

Although NASCAR drivers would not be familiar with teachings such as Mahayana *paramitas* or other initially obscure notions, I hear them exemplify these teachings virtually every weekend. Their attitudes toward life and work share so many elements of Buddhism that when a driver says, "That's racing," I find myself thinking, "No, that's equanimity!"

Drivers thoroughly understand the place of *viriya*—effort and dedication—in life, and I think they would be amused to learn that our word "virile" comes from a Buddhist virtue of hard work. Taking a philosophical approach, Alan Kulwicki once told an interviewer, "I read somewhere, and I've always said, 'Work to *become*, not to acquire.' If you ever become what you set out to become, you will acquire everything you need or want in the process."[105] More directly, Buddy Baker, a colorful and plain-spoken former driver, said, "I realized that anything worthwhile takes a lot of dedication, a lot of hard work."[106] Moreover, he explained the feeling that a driver has on winning his first race in terms of the work and the effort that went into it: "You can't explain it to the average person unless you just say, bottle up everything that you ever wanted to do and put it in some type of formula. That's what it's like for a race-car driver when he wins his first major race. The years that you worked getting there and the aggravation and everything is forgotten. It's like, okay, here's your peace pill. This will work for awhile."[107] But Dale Earnhardt Jr. is quick to follow that up with its natural (to a Buddhist, anyway) corollary about not clinging and renewing one's effort with each moment. He said of winning, "The joy of winning only prods you to work harder so that you might be lucky enough to feel that same thing next week."[108] You won? That's great! Now get back to the drawing board for next week, and start setting the car up for a whole new track. You had a moment of enlightenment? That's great! Now return to the meditation cushion, because this is a whole new moment, and you can begin your search for enlightenment all over again.

Junior's dad had a more specific take on effort in racing: "Finishing races is important, but racing is more important."[109] This attitude made Earnhardt a racer rather than simply a driver. He could look at the big picture and see that consistent finishes mattered for championship points, but once he was in the car, there was no moment in which he was giving less than his all. To him, the sport was not collecting championships. It was racing, blowing the doors off another car, giving an opponent a touch of the "chrome horn" (i.e., bumping them). After he was fined for using his bumper to nudge another driver out of the way—and coincidentally into the wall—Earnhardt famously asked, "If you ain't supposed to bump with them, why do they call 'em bumpers?" He was known for an attitude of "checkers or wreckers," meaning that he would either win or wreck trying, and in the sport of racing, he was willing to use up everything necessary—himself, his car, and even *your* car if need be—in order to get the win. Some people cursed at that, some cheered, and some simply shook their heads in disbelief, but everybody knew that Dale believed in putting forth an effort. Former racing journalist Ronda Rich commented, "Earnhardt is my role model for how success springs up...when passion is combined with action. Aspiring writers frequently ask me for advice on how to be published. They insist that writing is their passion and they want to write for a living, but very few will persevere and follow through. Their passion is worthless without action."[110] Of course, "action" could easily be replaced here with "effort," since she essentially means the same thing.

Two classic takes on NASCAR effort, though, come from two old-school drivers now retired, Buddy Baker and Dick Trickle (a driver of modest success who has nonetheless become famous far and wide in lists of strange sports names). Baker observed with his typical combination of sagacity and spirit, "When you need to excel or try to excel and you hear a guy say, 'Well, I had a fifth-place car and I drove it to fifth'—that's the same as saying, 'I'm happy with fifth place.' Nah, I like to hear a guy say, 'I took a fifth-place car and ran second with it.' To me, that's important. That old half-full, half-empty crap: I mean, c'mon. You still got half a glass—keep pouring."[111] And Dick Trickle summed it all up beautifully. His philosophy? As a Zen teacher might say, just this: "Ya gotta wanna."[112]

9

ONE-POINTED CONCENTRATION

You are empty—happily, peacefully empty—
of everything but the present moment.[113]

Another of the six Mahayana *paramitas* is *dhyana*, or one-pointed concentration. In Zen practice, this concentration is called *samadhi*, or being at one with the object of awareness. It is achieved when the observer consciousness, or monkey mind, is shut down, when we are completely absorbed in the task or idea before us. In such a state, we are less self-conscious but more holistic, according to Andrew Cooper, a Buddhist commentator who reflects on the spiritual side of sports. He alludes to Mihaly Csikszentmihalyi's definition of flow as "the merging of action and awareness" and elaborates upon that theme, adding,

> Concentration on a task frees up psychic energy that would otherwise be focused on the self and its myriad concerns.... When we operate in an integral fashion—with the whole body and the whole mind—we cease to be aware of the sense of self. And greater freedom from the self means greater freedom *for* the self.... The less self-conscious we are, the more conscious we become. The less self-centered we are, the more centered we become. In the words of the great medieval Christian mystic Meister Eckhart: "The truth is that the more ourselves we are, the less self is in us."[114]

This is the great and beautiful paradox of selflessness—that we become truer to our real nature when we try to overcome our false nature, the one that seeks comfort and clings to pleasure, even though the false nature is the one that is with us throughout each day, each hour, and each year of our lives. Many people can be fooled into thinking that it *is* their real nature. For those who see the glimmers of the buried jewel, though, those who sense their deep impatience with entertainment and day-to-day distractions, it is liberating to read Buddhist texts, or the works of many great Western thinkers who discovered the same truths, and to find that there is another way.

It occurs to me that this recognition of the truer, deeper self is the source, too, of race-car drivers' fearlessness. Speeds reaching 200 miles per hour, inches away from other cars, even periodically making contact with them, demand total concentration. Not only one's whole mind, but every fiber of one's being must be immersed in the task of racing, and because of this full focus, there is no ego left over to comment on how dangerous it all is. Fear is the luxury of a not-totally-occupied mind. Soldiers in battle speak of the same feeling, the feeling that they simply did what needed to be done and did not think at the time of the danger they were in. Too much of themselves was given over to the task to "think about" much of anything, and there is simply no room for fear. As Cooper points out, time spent in this state strengthens us as people, makes us more centered and more conscious. Many athletes or thrill-seekers, like gamblers, describe it in terms of "I've never felt more *alive.*" The practice of Buddhism aims at bringing such moments of full, engaged, *alive* immersion in the present into every moment of our lives. Buddhists may seem simple and peaceful on the surface, even laid back to the point of being disengaged, but the disengagement is only with the distractions and discursive thought of life. Beneath the surface is a profound, calm (yet intense) engagement with life just as it is, whether they are driving a race car, going through pain or grief, walking to work, or simply breathing and existing in line with our highest ideals.

In her book *Everyday Zen*, Charlotte Joko Beck makes explicit the similar demands of enlightenment and athletics when she says, "It's that kind of attention which is necessary for our Zen practice. We call it *samadhi*, this total oneness with the object.... This is the oneness of any great art, the great athlete, the person who passes well on the football field, the person who does well on the basketball court, anybody like that who has to learn to pay attention. It's that kind of *samadhi*."[115] Despite NASCAR's rise in popularity, I think the typical American focus on traditional team sports such as baseball, basketball, and football has led most commentators to overlook auto racing, which I believe is the sport that in its relentlessness and danger is the most likely to give athletes flow, *samadhi*, and ultimately the potential for a particularly southern and rural kind of enlightenment. Not that the other sports do not—any athlete in the moment of performance is intensely absorbed in it. But the "moment" of racing performance is hours long and largely uninterrupted; there are no halftimes or breaks between innings. Unlike baseball, basketball, and football players, who leave the field or court to rest at identifiable intervals, the race-car driver is constantly in the race and always on the track, even during a pit stop, when most drivers discuss changes to the car with their crew chief.

It is not necessary for race-car drivers to feel any fear. Some don't, or at least maintain that they do not. Earnhardt was asked what was the most fear he had ever felt in a race car, and he replied, "I've never been scared in a race car—*concerned*, maybe, but never scared." It was an answer in turn mischievous, sly, and true. It has the feel of a country joke about it, the playfulness with words that marks most southern humor, but also a bit of macho swagger and classic Earnhardt intimidation of any competitor who might confess to fear. Finally, on some levels, it was also perfectly true—there is no time in a race car to be afraid of anything, just enough time to think, "Hmm, this might not turn out too well."

On those occasions when a driver—or anyone else—does feel fear, he or she can keep in mind a story from Tibetan teacher Chögyam Trungpa Rinpoche's life. The rinpoche (an honorific title in Tibetan Buddhism) was entering a monastery with two attendants. A snarling guard dog, a huge Tibetan mastiff, was chained in the monastery yard. It was barking and growling at the strangers and generally acting quite ferocious. Suddenly, its chain came loose, and the dog lunged at the trio. Terrified, the attendants dashed toward the monastery doors. Rinpoche faced the dog for a moment, then took a deep breath and ran—straight toward the dog. The mastiff was so startled that it wheeled around and fled. Pema Chödrön tells this story to show how we learn how to push beyond the edge when we run up against our personal limits. We may meet our match with a poodle or with a belligerent guard dog, she says, but either way, the question is this: Which way do we run?[116]

Compare Chödrön's story and her question to what an observer said of Earnhardt and his ability to drive fearlessly through a screen of smoke in a wreck:

> And [Dale] has two abilities you have to have in this sport. First of all, he can leave the race at the track when he gets in his van and drives away. The race is over, it's history, and he can leave that, totally remove himself from it.
>
> And the other thing, Dale never looks to tomorrow. He plans that day, lives that day, and then when tomorrow comes, he lives that. As a result, his fear factor is so superior to

> any of the other drivers out there.... His attitude is, "Whatever happens, happens."... Dale has no fear. If you have a screen of smoke in front of you and you don't know what's on the other side, if you have ten people, three will step through it and seven won't.
>
> And because of his attitude about life, Dale doesn't feel any pressure. The pressure doesn't get to him like it does a guy who wonders and worries about the Sunday race on Friday. Dale takes each day as it comes, adapts to it and goes on, and it's a good philosophy if you can do it.[117]

It was wise of the commentator to add "if you can do it" because that kind of equanimity is difficult to master. It takes many years of practicing Buddhism to get to that point, and there are hundreds of Buddhist teachers across America and shelves full of books trying to help students reach just that state. Twenty years of racing, though, gave it to Earnhardt instinctively. He understood that this state was the best way to face life and to enjoy it day to day without undermining each moment with either fear or desire. Whether it's a guard dog or a screen of smoke from spinning cars, or whether it's the pressures you face in your own life and the edges that you run up against, the things that push your buttons, the question is the same: Which way do you run?

Two other things to note: We may find it easy, even pleasant, to practice letting go of negative events. But to live without clinging means also to let go of positive events as well. As the observer said of Earnhardt, live each day, let that day go, and live the next. It is wise not to cling to fear and drag ourselves down, but it is equally wise not to cling to pleasure and thus spoil ourselves and lose our discipline. Another point: The observer, a veteran race team manager as well as a childhood friend of Earnhardt, singles out in his assessment no less than four of the attributes we have discussed here—live in the present, let go of events when they are finished, do not be held hostage by your discursive thoughts, and be fearless (i.e., Do you drive through the smoke or don't you? Which way do you run?).

Reflecting on the balance we should maintain between focusing on this moment and keeping in mind the greater goal, Joseph Goldstein cites mountain climber Rene Daumal's commentary on staying focused. In *Mount Analogue* Daumal reminds mountain climbers to take each step mindfully while keeping the summit in sight: "Keep your eye fixed on the way to the top, but don't forget to look right in front of you. The last step depends on the first. Don't think you've arrived just because you see the summit. Watch your footing, be sure of the next step, but don't let that distract you from the highest goal. The first step depends on the last."[118] Goldstein goes on to comment that it may be our vision of the summit that inspires our journey, but being inspired and getting there are not the same thing.

He also makes an excellent point about doubt. When one-pointed concentration fails and that nagging observer mind is heard again, self-doubt can creep in, often just in time to distract us from victory:

> The first step is to recognize when the doubting mind is present and, in recognizing this, to become familiar with its various voices. If we become aware of these voices as mental tapes, simply more thoughts in the mind, we're less likely to become ensnared by their content. In that moment, we cease to give them power: "I can't do this" becomes just another thought. We can then bring wisdom to bear on the process of doubt itself, noticing how it takes us away from the direct experience of the moment.[119]

In other words, doubt that we can accomplish a goal can distract us at the very moment we *are* accomplishing it by insinuating itself as a negative running commentary in our heads. If we heed the doubting mind that says "I can't do this," we stop our efforts right there and make that very self-defeating prediction come true. If we simply continue with our actions, we are in fact pulling off exactly what we might be telling ourselves we can't accomplish. A Tibetan lama, like so many Tibetan refugees, walked all the way from Tibet to India through the snows of a Himalayan winter, a trek that can reach 300 miles. Asked how he managed it, he replied, "One step at a time."

Concentration, though, does more than push out fear and doubt. In being absorbed in the moment, we are clearing and stilling our minds and touching our spiritual essence, our essential clarity and calm. Drivers understand this kind of absorption well. Identifying his calming and focusing ritual before a race, Earnhardt Jr. wrote, "The world now moves in slow motion. Everything is quiet. I'm focused totally on the job ahead and I'm oblivious to the colorful pre-race activities. National anthem. Prayer. Military jet fly-over. Crazed cheers from the stands. I don't notice any of it today."[120] Even in the first race of his rookie season, he had mastered the skill of *dhyana*, one-pointed concentration, and he knows that a clear mind means a steady will.

The relationship between driver and crew chief is in some ways not unlike the one between Zen student and teacher. As noted, crew chiefs (and also spotters, the guys with walkie-talkies stationed on top of the tallest seating tower, whose job is to watch for trouble on the track and warn the driver) will talk a driver through moments where he might lose his concentration or panic. Sometimes the crew chief or spotter acts as a cheerleader to boost a driver's confidence, but more often, the driver has plenty of confidence and altogether too much passion. The crew chief and spotter act to calm him and redirect his mind to just this moment, just this lap, just this breath. In their instructions to the driver, they are balanced between being calming and supportive, and they work hard to keep the driver's doubting observer mind silenced so that the driver can race. Veteran crew chief Jeff Hammond observed, "The driver is in a world of his own, isolated for three and a half to four hours. He is totally concentrating on driving the race car, and his only connection to the outside world…is the guy on the other end of the radio."[121]

As for the intensity of that kind of concentration, driver Kenny Wallace uses an interesting phrase. Racing, he says, has "the element of misery" in it. "This sport requires the element of misery whether you like it or not. It took me a long time to realize that and Rusty [Kenny's older brother, also a veteran driver] had it figured out from the day he jumped into a race car. I did not realize in competition how some people, if they don't win at all, they feel like they're failures. I feel like if I'm a player, and I get a chance to win every time, that's what makes me happy."[122] Wallace's use of the word "misery" shows that not every driver arrives completely at the sense of wisdom and equanimity that I hope they do, perhaps because wrong motivation keeps them thinking of trophies instead of racing as a path to wisdom and as pure love of competition.

One-pointed concentration is, I think, at least a part of what Earnhardt meant when he said that finishing races was important, but racing was more important. There are times when all a driver can see is that next pass, and in that moment the race definitely is a matter of checkers or wreckers. He said, "You race like hell over the last ten laps until you cross the finish line or you turn over somewhere."[123] He was willing to take either of those outcomes, but he was not willing to take second place. He was asked once "what kind of a sensation is it" to go three-wide into turn three, racing furiously. He answered cheerfully, "It's a great feeling if you come out of turn three!"[124] What made Earnhardt special was that he threw himself completely into the moment, completely into racing. He didn't always know how things would turn out, even in the next split-second, but he fearlessly trusted in his abilities and his efforts to carry him through. More often than not, they did. After all, one thing about laser-like focus that every racer understands is this: The last lap is the only one worth leading.

10

EQUANIMITY; OR, THAT'S RACIN'

I've been criticized enough where y'all can't hurt me. You can't write anything that's going to make my day any worse. And you can't, all of a sudden, tell me I'm smart and great and make me feel any better. I didn't believe you when you said I sucked, and I'm not going to believe you when you say I'm great!

—Michael Waltrip[125]

Two of the most important traits that I believe Buddhists and race-car drivers share are equanimity and acceptance of death. Equanimity is defined as evenness of mind, composure, balance, and a mindfulness that is not easily rattled. Equanimous people are the ones who are the eye of the storm, those who stay calm in the midst of chaos. In Buddhist terms, equanimity is the quality (and the practice) of being centered, subject to neither clinging nor its opposite, aversion. Here is part of a brief discourse on equanimity: "You hear some bad news. Immediately your heart pounds, your breath tightens, your face frowns. You hear some good news. Your heart jumps, your face smiles. In both cases, your thoughts swirl and you lose your center. You see something disgusting, you feel pain, you notice a horrible thought...and you lose your center, rushing toward or fleeing from what you have encountered. All this describes our ordinary mode of...automated, conditioned...living."[126]

Equanimity is usually contrasted with reactivity. Reactivity is the ordinary state of continually responding to events and stimuli (particularly trivial stimuli or events that do not affect us). Equanimity, on the other hand, consists of maintaining a calmly centered presence rather than allowing the quality of our days and our minds to be determined by random events. A state of centered calm leaves room for events and feelings both wanted and unwanted, allowing such things to have their "space" without also allowing them to have control of our minds. A particularly good formulation I have found is this: "equanimity enables us to meet life with aplomb."[127]

Equanimity is also expressed in self-help slogans such as "the wisdom of allowing" and "saying yes to life." It strikes me that the large majority of the self-help sections in bookstores these days consist of dumbing down complex and vitally interrelated Buddhist concepts into stand-alone slogans aimed at the sitcom-watching audience. While I am glad that the concepts get any consideration in America at all, I wince at seeing them taken out of their context in the Buddhist path, where each concept supports and underlies the rest.

In fact, I hope you are beginning to realize that in order to practice equanimity—to really experience the *lived* effect of it—you would also have to incorporate discipline, patience, mindfulness, and an understanding of impermanence. It takes all of these *paramitas* to reach equanimity, and once you have attained it, equanimity supports all of the others. I have previously compared Buddhism to a net, thoroughly linked together but with no linear progression and no apparent center. Each element knits together with the others to form a complete philosophy of behavior. As an example, I'll give you an incident from my own life, one that called upon everything I knew about Buddhism.

My husband and I retired when I was twenty-nine and he was thirty-two. We had both been working in the busy, crowded, expensive, stressful Northeast, and we were getting burned out. We had talked casually about moving back to my native rural Virginia one day, but the impetus, when it came, was dreadful.

One day, James called me at work and could say only, "Dave is dead." David Paul Trieloff, the brilliant, charismatic, funny heart of our college clique, was only thirty-two years old. He was loud and boisterous, and absolutely everyone who met him loved him immediately. No matter what flaws he might have had, his charm and wit were so great that his friends loved him anyway, and his heart was so large and generous that everyone else did too.

In retrospect, we could all see the signs that Dave's heart was failing—a sudden weight gain that left him looking bloated, complaints that he got winded easily, an increasing use of his asthma inhaler. But he was only thirty-two, so nobody really expected him to die. He died on a sunny April day, driving home from work, the victim of a massive heart attack. As a friend said at the funeral, the irony was that it was such a great heart. We didn't understand how it could have failed him, because it had never failed any of us.

It was another moment when impermanence truly comes home to you. We were not satisfied with our lives—and now we knew how brief a moment life really is. Six weeks later, we put our house on the market and prepared to move to Virginia.

Using the proceeds from a house that was within walking distance to the New York City train, we bought a huge, rambling Victorian fixer-upper in the small town of Staunton, Virginia. The house needed a total rehab—not all of the electricity worked, the attic was home to hundreds of pigeons (because parts of it were open to the sky), and chunks of plaster were falling from the ceilings. In our youth and innocence (okay, stupidity), we planned to park our extra money in the stock market and do all the work ourselves, living off the investments until the house was finished.

It was a plan—and during the roaring 1990s, when the NASDAQ neared 5,000, it worked beautifully. Despite the fact that we were using it for our living expenses as well as renovation costs, our investment grew wildly, peaking at $250,000. We were retired, in our early thirties, and getting as dirty as children every day, bringing a beautiful old home back from the brink.

Too bad we were in techs. The bubble burst. Every month, I called our broker, asking if she was sure we shouldn't cash out now, simply cut our losses and put what was left in bonds or cash. No, no, she said, ride it out—no need to sell at a loss; the market would bounce back. Of course, that was the conventional wisdom, especially of brokers too young to have ever seen anything but a bubble. It seemed reasonable at the time. She was the one with the license, and we trusted her. And, in all honesty, greed played a role. We liked being idle and a little bit rich, and we liked the huge profits that had been run up. We wanted to believe that they would come back.

Of course, they never did. The hemorrhaging finally stopped when our account was worth $2,000. Yep, we had lost $248,000. We both had to stop work on the house and find full-time jobs immediately. We held out as long as we could, to the bitter end as it turned out, but a small fortune—our only fortune—was gone, and it wasn't coming back.

At a moment like that, you can imagine that phrases such as "say yes to life" or "*allow* this" are not what you want to hear (which is why these stand-alone slogans do not seem as effective to me as the whole of Buddhism). And, sure, we were not exactly blissful over it. But what does anger get us? It doesn't magically turn the stock market around. It doesn't magically restore our fortunes. It only makes us unhappy. We feel wronged, aggrieved, put upon, and we want someone else to pay—if we carried that attitude around, we might find ourselves being aggressive with others, wanting to push off our suffering onto them, to make them suffer more so that we can suffer less. We might be caught up in judging our broker, although she was doing the best she could without the benefit of seeing the future, and if we carry that attitude around, we reinforce habits of being judgmental and feeling superior, habits neither of us wants to cultivate and habits that are not traits of the Eightfold Path. We might have felt guilty about our own avarice in wanting to stay retired, but guilt does not change the past. It only poisons the present.

Many people marveled at how well we took the loss, shaking their heads as they told us so. "Boy, if it were me..." they said, trailing off with another head shake.

But before we had sold the house in New Jersey, we had considered the possibility of failure. What would happen if everything went wrong? Well, we would wind up in a house that was not fixed up, out of money, and we would need to get jobs. But in the meantime, we had moved to a quieter, more peaceful town, acquired a lower cost of living, and spent three years in happy retirement, at least partially saving a historic home. That wasn't really a bad "failure," was it? It didn't seem that way to us, anyway—and that was the worst-case scenario. Not knowing that a stock bubble was about to burst, we foresaw at least an equal chance that we would finish the house, sell it, and begin building a tiny empire of renovated homes. Either way, we had reevaluated our lives after Dave's death, and we had acted on that reevaluation—we had gone for the peace and the joy, and, even in abject "failure," we had achieved them. So we had to work now—we'd had to work before, in the Northeast. If we had never moved, we would never have had the time off that we did, or the adventure. So we had failed. Big deal.

Don't get me wrong—I like money. Money means security. It means not worrying. I did a lot of worrying about bills when we were down to our last $2,000 (and the house still cost $600 a month to heat in the winter). But the loss of pretty much all of our money forced me to reevaluate my feelings about money and security as well. The money was gone, but I was still here, and I was still as much at peace with my decision as I had been before. During those three years off, we had rescued a newborn kitten abandoned by its mother, gotten married, hiked the Grand Canyon, and taken one dream vacation to Japan (if not for that trip, we might have bottomed out at $4,000 instead of two, but it was worth it). All of it was worth it. I did a lot of thinking about my attitude toward money, and I realized that one thing that was *not* worth it was letting money interfere with my equanimity, my mindfulness, my resilience, and my joy.

Maintaining equanimity meant seeing what happened with bare awareness, without storytelling or judging. Instead of "the money is gone because we shouldn't have been in techs and our broker was too young and why oh why weren't we in bonds and why didn't we stay up North," there was simply the recognition, "the money is gone—what now?" None of the rest of it really mattered anyway. Stick to the essentials if you want a clear mind.

Keeping our equanimity also meant having the discipline to acknowledge the tendency to anger and judging without following those thoughts and being caught up in them. To have that discipline, we also had to have the mindfulness to observe our thoughts and see them as thoughts before reacting to them. In a way, the thought almost has to be seen and felt as a foreign object in the mind rather than as our own voice in our heads, part of us.

We had to be patient (to practice *kshanti*) and to manage our disappointment; and it helps to have that attitude of "the glass is already broken." Years ago, a car we had owned caught fire all by itself and burned, something the firefighters on the scene said sometimes happened with older cars. My husband later wrote a haiku to the effect that the car had all along borne the seeds of its own destruction. Even before he had really heard of the concept of impermanence from me and my Buddhist practice, he grasped it intuitively. In the long term, the glass was already broken, the car was already on fire, and the money was already gone—the actual moment had to arrive sooner or later, and it happened that the bursting of the tech bubble was the moment it arrived. Or, as John Maynard Keynes observed about long-term economic forecasts, "In the long term, we're all dead." So we coped with the death of a beloved friend and the loss of our entire savings by using discipline, bare awareness, an understanding of impermanence, patience, a little true love, and a lot of humor.

All the elements of Buddhism that we have discussed weave together to form a cohesive, comprehensive path, a way of dealing with everything that life throws at us. This is why Buddhists say that daily life is our path and that all things are practice. Since mindfulness is new in every moment and since impermanence renews the opportunity for enlightenment every moment, there is not a minute a day when we can avoid practice. This constant pressure to be aware may seem effortful, but the best way to approach it is to relax into the practice. When the practice is something you do routinely, like wearing clothes, then you are embodying your understanding, moment to moment. That is the goal: to get the daily lived experience of *sukha*, not merely the intellectual understanding of it.

NASCAR drivers have their own distinctive version of equanimity. It's the phrase "That's racing," repeated without fail by somebody every race weekend. It encompasses everything from wrecking someone else, whether inadvertently or on purpose, getting wrecked, whether inadvertently or on purpose, having a great race car sidelined by a part failure, having a lousy race car, and pretty much any other conceivable racing situation. The phrase encompasses *all* of racing, and its meaning is this: "There's nothing you can do about it. Get over it and move on." "That's racing" is the drivers' way of handling the unexpected bad breaks that strike in the middle of a nice sunny summer afternoon at the track.

The 1990 Daytona 500, the one that Earnhardt lost when his tire blew on the last turn of the last lap, was admittedly the biggest disappointment of his career. Richard Childress, the owner of Earnhardt's car and Earnhardt's best friend, said of the loss, "What a heartbreaker. To be a half-mile from something you've dreamed about all your life…man, that's awfully hard to take. But that's racing. It'll bite you when you least expect it."[128] There was nothing else to say but "that's racing," and Childress and Earnhardt had already dealt with it. Rather than dwelling on the heartbreak, they moved immediately to the philosophical verbal shrug of "that's racing," and they packed up, went home, and got ready to go racing again the following weekend. The payoff for being able to move past the defeat? Earnhardt won his fourth championship that year, on his way to seven, all told.

I wonder sometimes whether drivers ever consider the irony of the fact that they drive 500 miles and yet end up in exactly the same place they started, not even venturing outside the circumference of the track. Whether they think of it consciously or not, I think they intuitively feel the underlying sense of irony and emptiness, and maybe this feeling helps them to let it go when they have misfortune. At the same time, Earnhardt once observed that it was 500 miles and sometimes you won by mere inches. To get each precious inch, there was no moment that you didn't have to give it your all, so racing is a balancing act between throwing your whole body, mind, and soul into driving, and then being able to shrug and say "that's racing" when your body, mind, soul, and car end up in the wall. The practice of Zen also recognizes the human desire to cling to more pleasant possibilities or, as Charlotte Joko Beck describes them, other "if onlies": "There are many people in the world who feel that if only they had a bigger car, a nicer house, better vacations, a more understanding boss, or a more interesting partner, then their life would work. We all go through that one. Slowly we wear out most of our 'if onlies.'... Coming into a practice like Zen, we bring our usual notions that we are going to get somewhere—get enlightened—and get all the cookies that have eluded us in the past."[129] In NASCAR, "that's racing" is a way of giving up the "if onlies" of racing and accepting the "it happens."

Drivers also say that you have to learn to lose before you can learn to win. Few drivers will ever win their first time out, and to get to the top level of NASCAR a driver races hundreds of times. His record may be stellar, but he still must lose more often than he wins. Everybody knows that Babe Ruth hit 714 home runs, but few remember that he also struck out 1,330 times. If Babe Ruth had gotten discouraged by losing, he would never have made it to the major leagues; and if drivers had felt defeated by losing a few or even several races, they would never have made it to the NASCAR circuit.

Drivers understand equanimity in myriad ways. Buddy Baker observes, "People don't understand when a guy gets out of the car after a race and goes after another driver. They don't realize these are spirited people, or they wouldn't be able to do what they do."[130]

That is true, but it is also a relatively rare occurrence anymore. While longtime fans blame the current infrequency of post-race showdowns on drivers who are increasingly corporate shills, the truth is that it is also a case of drivers managing their minds more carefully. Having cultivated equanimity for years, they find themselves reaching for it habitually. Dale Jr. quoted his father when he said, "Racing is going and doing. Things happen."[131] Earnhardt understood that racing was all action. Not every action could turn out exactly as he planned, and with forty-two other drivers planning actions, not every action might be one he wanted. Whatever happened in a split second, he did what he needed to do, moved on, and did not waste time getting upset. He had too much "going and doing" still ahead of him to worry about what had gone and been done before.

For the most part, NASCAR drivers maintain equanimity in the face of media scrutiny and even having their talents and motivations judged in print by near strangers. When people began questioning whether he could still drive anymore, an aging Terry Labonte quipped, "I never said I *could* drive."[132] Easygoing Carl Edwards told the media, "I just want to thank you guys because you've written some really nice things about me…and I know it won't always be good. There'll be times when you have to write bad things about me, and I'll be grateful for that, too."[133] While drivers are served by getting good publicity and appearing to be nice guys, I do not think this attitude is merely a façade on their parts, for two reasons. First, this attitude of acceptance and appreciation makes a hectic life with a lot of pressures easier to deal with. They can't obsess over every word written about them or every tap from someone else's bumper. Drivers simply do not have the time to worry about such things. Second, people whose mindset is *not* one of equanimity can rarely fake it. The words "that's racing," or whatever the equivalent, do not spring readily to their lips. Neither driver had a PR person standing at his elbow whispering the most media-savvy words to him. The drivers responded off the cuff and with the natural ease and good humor that equanimity provides.

In the most traumatic moments, our equanimity is unavoidably shaken, even temporarily destroyed. To have it be otherwise would mean that we were cold and unfeeling. Buddhists would never expect someone who has suffered the death of a loved one to shrug it off. But their way of dealing with grief or other devastating setbacks is healthier than Western ways of mourning. Buddhists say, "Take time out and really feel this fully. Sit with the feeling. Don't run away from it. Grieve 100 percent. Hurt 100 percent. Cry 100 percent. But when you've done that, realize that you're finished. You've done 100 percent and cannot do more. Don't cling to the hurt and make it your companion. Don't fetishize it and make it your nemesis. Give it 100 percent, and then realize that it cannot be changed and move forward."

It isn't easy to practice that way of grieving, but I know from experience that it works, and there is a stunning example of it in racing. Most of America has seen replays of the moment of Dale Earnhardt's death, the awful silence of the wrecked car settling into the infield. The car right ahead of him, watching the wreck unfold in his rearview mirror, was driven by his son. Witnessed by millions, Dale Jr. watched his father die right before his eyes. My own father died when I was nineteen, and even then, I cannot imagine what Junior went through in that moment. On top of that, he had to return to Daytona, twice a year every year, and race there himself. He could not fetishize the track and say, "I can't bear to be in that place. I refuse to go there." And he absolutely could not make that pain his companion, or he would never be able to drive a race car again for thinking about it.

So when the time came to go back, Dale Jr. went to Daytona one day when the track was empty, with a few people close to him. He walked to the spot of his father's impact, sat down, and just thought. He said he sat there for nearly an hour, thinking about his dad and going through all the feelings he needed to go through. When he stood up, he said, he knew he would be able to race there again. Equanimity may be easiest to explain when it comes to letting go of a minor event, but this is equanimity in the face of personal, life-changing catastrophe. It hurts to do it, but it is disastrous not to do it.

Western culture sometimes tells us to "cowboy up," to be strong and push the pain down. But if it is not dealt with completely, it is not gone, and it will haunt us for years, warping our personalities as we try to avoid it, repress it, ignore it, distract ourselves, and do anything not to feel it. More and more, the swallowed pain starts to feel like a bottomless pit, one that we don't dare to look at closely or get too near. But when we approach it as Dale Jr. did, sitting down next to that deadly wall and facing what hurts the most, we are surprised to find that the pain does have a stopping point. When we have felt all the hurt we have, we know intuitively that we are done, that we have finished grieving. Then, we can get up and move on, and instead of "cowboying up," we really are strong again. The Buddhist teaching for experiencing grief corresponds to its teaching about experiencing joy: Live it fully. Don't dilute joy with worries or clinging, and don't dilute grief by distracting yourself from it. Live each moment, as it comes, to its fullest, good and bad.

Bobby Allison had found his equanimity in the face of tragedy when he told journalist Ronda Rich that if he were not willing to question the good in life, he didn't feel he could question the bad. From Allison, Rich learned about equanimity and managing one's mind. As she puts it, "From him, I learned that if we are to triumph over a life that sometimes seeks to defeat us, we must *choose* courage. Courage doesn't come by chance.... From Bobby's example, I learned that the mind can be a powerful ally or a destructive adversary.... For how we believe is how we behave."[134] Rich gets her understanding about the power of the mind from Bobby Allison, but there is a similar teaching in Buddhism. In *The Teaching of Buddha*, the phrasing reads, "A man's mind may make him a Buddha, or it may make him a beast. Misled by error, one becomes a demon; enlightened, one becomes a Buddha. Therefore, control your mind and do not let it deviate from the right path."[135] But controlling the mind does not mean being unfeeling or indifferent. On the contrary, it means feeling things completely, until they are drained from us, rather than repressing them and allowing them to remain with us for years, unsettling our balance. Controlling the mind means seeing our thoughts as ephemeral, living up to our highest ideals moment to moment and being aware (but forgiving) of moments we do not, and approaching every task with absorption, then letting go completely so that we can be fully receptive to the next moment.

Not only did Rich learn about balance and mental discipline from Allison, but she also learned about karma from other drivers. Specifically, she recalls, "From many of my racing friends like Earnhardt, Childress, the Martins, the Pettys, and the Elliotts, I learned how to behave when life blesses you. Good follows good and bad follows bad. The seeds of kindness, compassion, and goodwill produce a harvest of the same."[136] "Good follows good and bad follows bad" is an accurate, practical definition of karma.

We practice equanimity because we want a harvest of peace, and we will not get it from being reactive.

Thankfully, though, most of our trials are not those of deep trauma, but of day-to-day annoyances. For drivers, there might be the loss of a $75,000 race car, but still, "that's racing." Earnhardt was remarkably philosophical about loss—perhaps fitting for a man who was once photographed, grinning mischievously, beside a towering pile of the sheet metal he had destroyed over a single season. About wrecking, he said, "Sure, it was frustrating to be running up front and not winning. But part of racing is that to be a good winner, you've got to be a good loser." He said of another Daytona heartbreaker (in which he ran out of gas with three laps to go after leading for most of the day), "I can take losing just like I can take winning. Ain't nothing to complain about."[137] Or as it is expressed in an unattributed quotation in *1000 Paths to Wisdom*, "You win some, you lose some, you wreck some." At the moment I saw the quote, I laughed aloud because although the book did not say, I knew exactly who had said it: NASCAR's own favorite son, Dale Earnhardt.

One might say that Earnhardt was not being philosophical as much as stoic, simply suffering in silence. But I don't think so, because he also appreciated the good that came along, saying, "You can't let one bad moment spoil a bunch of good ones."[138] He never lost his awareness or appreciation for the good moments. He practiced equanimity.

11

ACCEPTING DEATH, EMBRACING LIFE

> One cannot get away from fate. If a person does not fulfill his nature, he will lead a frustrated life and be unhappy. If it involves him in fear he will just have to put up with it.
>
> —Sir Francis Chichester[139]

In *Buddhism without Beliefs*, Stephen Batchelor asks us to deeply consider this question: "Since death alone is certain and the time of death uncertain, what should I do?"[140] Obviously, it is a question about how we choose to live, how we set our priorities. Most people can avoid framing the question in such blunt terms as death. They prefer to frame it in terms of what color their parachute is, or what their family and career goals are, or what they want to do when they retire.

Buddhists and race-car drivers actually frame the question pretty much exactly as Batchelor puts it: in terms of our own imminent death—Buddhists because that is the traditional practice we've learned and race-car drivers because they have no other choice. They have chosen a sport in which death may happen in almost any second, so they must live as though their time on earth is limited and precious. Buddhists behave the same way, as do those who have survived a brush with death. Most people agree that, in theory, we should all be that way, but normal daily life does not offer clear techniques to support that philosophy, so it must be acquired via some thread in that tapestry of higher consciousness as I suggested in the introduction.

Earnhardt's death in 2001 was one of a string of five deaths in just over a year, a particularly bad run for NASCAR. The other four were Adam Petty (the youngest member of the Petty dynasty), Kenny Irwin, Tony Roper, and Blaise Alexander. However, racing had been a far more dangerous sport in its heyday of the 1950s and 1960s. With drivers racing as often as three or four times a week in smaller venues, it was not uncommon for a driver to attend five or more funerals *every* year. Drivers had to face not only their own potential death, but the very real deaths of friends, rivals, and brothers-in-arms. Worse yet, since NASCAR has always been a family sport, with brothers and sons following older relatives into the sport and many families marrying into other racing families, sometimes the death was of a son, a father, a brother, a cousin, or family related by marriage. As a result, decades' worth of race-car drivers have had to come to terms with death, to come to accept its proximity, or to come to an accommodation with it one way or another, understanding its place at the deep, dark heart of the life they lived with such passion.

NASCAR historian Peter Golenbock said, "To a man, what they loved to do more than anything else on earth—including eating, wenching, or fishing—was to drive that race car fast.... To be part of this made them feel vibrant, alive—feelings they never took for granted."[141] They never did take the joy in their lives for granted, but they balanced that with a matter-of-fact acceptance of death's reality. For example, veteran driver David Pearson said in an interview, "I never did think about danger. Never did. It never did enter my mind about that part of it. If you get to thinking about something like that, that it's dangerous, you're not going to run as good as you can, you ain't gonna have a hundred percent in it. If you're scared, afraid something is going to happen to you, before you know it someone is going to outrun you."[142]

Pearson approached racing like a soldier in battle. He was too fully absorbed in what he was doing to leave any leftover ego commenting on the element of danger, and when he was off the track he simply blocked out such thoughts. Many more drivers, though, simply seem to have a fatalistic acceptance that they could die tomorrow. The distinction is that they know this fact without fearing it. Pearson speaks of thinking about danger as fearing it, but men like Earnhardt thought about it without fear. So it seems to work out this way for a driver: If you don't know you're in danger, you're okay—although many drivers might say you're stupid. If you know it and don't fear it, you're okay. But if you know it and fear it, you're done for. Life is pretty much the same way: If you undertake a new task, career, or project without ever thinking that you could fail, you'll be okay. If you think about the possibility of failure and accept that although it might happen you do not fear it, then you'll be all right. But if you embark on a new project and fear failure, odds are that you will never see that project through successfully or completely.

Richard Petty and Dale Earnhardt have been described as the alpha and omega of NASCAR racing—both seven-time champions (tied for the most) and both legends, the two most recognizable names in the sport. Petty was the ever-smiling, friendly driver who followed his father Lee into racing and built an empire. He was perhaps not the most naturally talented guy behind the wheel, but he took care of his equipment, raced smart, and worked hard. Earnhardt also followed his father into racing, but having dropped out of school, married at eighteen, and fathered children young, his career took a detour through grinding poverty before he built his own empire. Earnhardt was gruff, so gruff that a promoter who arranged a cocktail party in his honor remembers the evening this way: "Earnhardt sat on one side of the room and the fans sat on the other.... Even the ones bold enough to go over and get their pictures taken with Earnhardt would pose with him quickly and then move on—as if they were all afraid he was going to punch them."[143] Certainly, that's one way to live up to his nickname of "The Intimidator." Nevertheless, Earnhardt possessed a raw, astonishing talent, so much so that many commentators called him the greatest driver ever to turn a steering wheel.

Both the Petty and the Earnhardt dynasties have also suffered their share of racing tragedy. Richard's brother Maurice quotes their father's devoutly religious fatalism, one shared by his descendants: "Hey, to quote Mr. Lee Petty, 'Every hair on your head is counted, and when it's your day, it's your day.' If you're in this game, that's the only way you better be thinking about it."[144] For the Pettys, their most recent tragedies struck almost simultaneously. Patriarch Lee Petty died at the age of eighty-six on April 5, 2000. A life well and fully lived, and perhaps not so much a tragedy, but just a month later, his nineteen-year-old great-grandson Adam, son of Kyle and grandson of Richard, died in a practice session at New Hampshire Speedway, the victim of a stuck throttle that propelled him into a wall at full speed. Thus, the only four-generation racing family in NASCAR history lost the bookends of those four generations within a few weeks.

Adam's family memorialized him in a wonderful way by creating a racing-themed summer camp for sick children. That helped them focus and deal with their grief. Eventually his father Kyle could say, "We just look at it that part of living is dying. Adam just got it a little bit earlier than when we wanted him to."[145] There is nothing callous about his statement—Kyle still feels his son's death deeply. He drove his son's car number from Adam's death in 2000 through the 2008 season, unwilling to let the dream of a continued Petty presence in NASCAR die. And in Adam's honor, Petty left the space above the door, where the driver's name always appears, blank, because he said he was only driving the car for his son, not for himself.

As for the Earnhardts, they suffered the singular fate of seeing their patriarch, with his force-of-nature personality, the center of gravity of their universe, die in front of them, while millions of viewers witnessed their anguish live. Of the Earnhardts who drove, Dale lost his father when he was twenty-two, and Dale Jr. was twenty-seven when he watched his father die in his rearview mirror, so they have not made it to thirty with a living father for two generations. Nor did Dale's car owner, Richard Childress, who lost his father at five and who bonded with Earnhardt partly over the shared trauma of being fatherless.

The Pettys' and Earnhardts' sadly truncated history reminds me of a Zen story quoted in the classic *Zen Flesh, Zen Bones.* A rich man asked an enlightened master to paint him a calligraphy scroll, one that would bestow an honor on his family that might be continued through the generations and ensure their future happiness. Sengai, the master, agreed. He took a large scroll and wrote, "Grandfather dies, father dies, son dies."

The rich man was enraged. "I asked you for a scroll for the happiness of my family, and you insult me with this joke!"

"No insult, no joke," replied Sengai. "If your son should die before you, that would grieve you greatly. If your grandson should die before you or your son, you would both be devastated. But if you die in the order I've written, generation after generation, then your family will have enjoyed true happiness."[146]

Culturally, we flirt with death. Like children at an adults' party, we sneak down the stairs and peek through the banister at it, then scurry away before we're caught. We play video games in which we die repeatedly, only to turn off the computer or game console and resume our daily living. We watch crime shows to see sudden, violent death and also to see it punished. Thus is the moral order of the universe restored, chaos held at bay for another weeknight hour. We bravely seek thrills, but then fearfully worship youth. Our heroes, whether they are sports stars or soldiers or firefighters, are people who genuinely do live closer to the edge than most of us do. We watch them carefully, hoping to see a glimpse, a hint, of how we should behave ourselves when that final moment comes. Racing fan L. D. Russell writes about our vicarious foretasting of death,

> Ours is a culture fascinated by death and starved in our guts for immortality. How many billions of dollars do we spend each year looking for ways to look and feel younger, to slow if not halt the aging process? How many simulated deaths occur on television and in movie theaters every single night of the week? We as viewers participate in these untimely ends, as if we might gain a foretaste of our own demise, a glimpse of what surely lies ahead for each and every one of us.[147]

He also says, "A noble, courageous death is the next best thing to rolling away the stone from the mouth of the tomb."[148] As every culture since at least the ancient Greeks has taught, a good death embodies our loftiest aspirations, even leading to a kind of immortality for the one brave enough to achieve it. As I quoted in the early pages of this book, "Character may be manifested in the great moments, but it is made in the small ones." A display of noble character at the moment of death allows us to assume (reverse-engineering, if you will) a noble life as well, and we understand intuitively that moments of great consequence, such as the end of life, are the truest indicators of what we have inside, our deepest inner nature. Our reactions in such moments are unguarded and truer than they will ever be at any other moment, and thus we are deeply impressed by a display of courage, grace, and dignity.

Most importantly, facing and accepting death leads to a sea change in one's attitude toward life. In this regard, monks and racers make a practice of straightforwardness toward death, but this practice is not limited to those who are marked out for religious or sporting life. This sea change is available to all of us. It is entirely possible for us to arrive at it through introspection and practice, but far more commonly we arrive at it through no choice of our own, through either the loss of family or a close friend or through an unexpected encounter with our own mortality. Buddhist teacher John Snelling says, "In order that life be tenable, most people suppress the reality and inevitability of death. Those who have been forced to confront it, however, will bear witness to the profound effect it can have. A vital shock it always is, but one that can also bring about a sudden maturing of the whole personality by summarily clearing the mind of its usual clutter of trivial preoccupations and bringing into focus that which is of real importance."[149]

This unadulterated mental space is the starting point for religious views of death. It should be approached with an attitude similar to St. Paul's "I have fought the good fight,"[150] and it should be considered in light of the character we aspire to have, a clear mind that sees what is truly important. Writer and meditation teacher Jack Kornfield asks, "At the end of life, when one has lived a life with some consciousness, one looks back, and the questions are so simple and basic: Did I live fully, and did I love well?"[151] Similarly, Buddhist monk Matthieu Ricard writes,

> The wise man enjoys a very special kind of freedom: prepared for death, he appreciates every moment of life's bounty. He lives each day as if it were his only one. That day naturally becomes the most precious of his existence. When he looks at the sunset, he wonders: "Will I see the sun rise again tomorrow morning?" He knows that he has no time to lose, that time is precious, and that it is foolish to waste it in idleness. When death finally comes for him, he dies tranquilly, without sadness or regret, without attachment to what he is leaving behind. He leaves this life as the eagle soars into the blue.[152]

Compare this enlightened perspective to Dale Earnhardt's casual comment, "You can't worry about tomorrow. Tomorrow may never come." Or compare it to what an observer said of Earnhardt, that he never planned for tomorrow, but simply lived each day as it came to him and then lived the next one when it got there. People with no grasp of Buddhism defined him clearly as a man who dwelt fully and mindfully in the present moment. I think this is true of many other drivers as well. The best-known and most beloved drivers of the 1950s and 1960s "golden age" were wild hell-raisers like Tiny Lund and Curtis Turner, men who both died young. However they approached their deaths, both lived their lives as fully as possible and saw life as too precious to be wasted in idleness. This attitude results from facing death, whether as a driver in a race car, as a patient in a cancer ward, or as a Buddhist in a meditation hall. This ability to embrace the inevitability and unpredictability of death in the midst of joyous daily living is why I believe that Buddhism and NASCAR share some transcendent DNA at their hearts.

Many years spent practicing, whether as an athlete or as one of Pema Chödrön's "spiritual warriors," yield a certain air of grace and contentment. Moreover, one seems to acquire perspective and gratitude for one's good fortune. Sportswriter Leigh Montville says of baseball great Cal Ripken, "The man seemed to have a sense of fulfillment in middle age, a completeness…to his life.… Excellence had brought him to a certain place, rich and famous, businesses everywhere, but longevity had brought him to another. He knew exactly how good his life was. He knew exactly what mattered."[153] Montville goes on to say that Earnhardt had acquired a similar attitude through his decades of racing. Nearing fifty, he was in the position of looking back and beginning to sum up a long and extraordinarily successful career, and beginning to speak more philosophically of life.

This is why *dukkha*, suffering, can come from both pleasure as well as pain. When life is good, we want to cling to our happiness, to deny the possibility that "tomorrow may never come." We want to reject impermanence and to skip *kshanti*, or patience, in the face of setbacks. We want to stay in the *samsaric* world of rewards and trophies and delight. We want perfection to last forever, even perfection in someone else's life, if we're a fan of theirs. But no matter how much we want permanent perfection, we cannot guarantee it, and therein lies our suffering. What we cling to is, inevitably, eventually taken away, and the only way to survive this loss is through some form of practice, some way to discipline our minds, accept loss, and let go of what we wanted so that we can move on with what we actually have.

During Speedweek 2001, Dale Earnhardt sat down in an empty garage with Darrell Waltrip, once a bitter rival but now an old friend, two aging southern men putting their feet up and talking about life. They joked about getting a rocking chair for Dale, who was beginning to look toward retirement, and speculated about the chance that before he retired he would win his record-breaking eighth championship. He had finished second in points the year before, was healthy and strong again after a lingering injury, and was fired up again with enthusiasm for the sport after having raced alongside his son during Dale Jr.'s rookie season. Dale was in a contented, introspective mood, and it was with a soft, boyish tone of wonder in his voice that he told Waltrip, "I'm doing a lot better today than I did several years ago. Because of family life. I'm a better person than I used to be. Great wife. Great family. I've really got it all right now. Racing. Winning. Competitive. Grandkids. I've got it all, Darrell. I got it all."[154]

Three days later, Dale Earnhardt died.

POSTLUDE

You don't get to choose how you're going to die. Or when. You can only decide how you're going to live. Now.
—Joan Baez[155]

I said at the outset that I wanted to show you how NASCAR drivers and Buddhists shared some traits, such as mindfulness, concentration, acceptance of impermanence (and through that, joyfulness in the present moment), and equanimity. I hope that I have done that, but rather more, I hope that I have shown you new ways to look at life. Whomever you admire, be it writers, football players, teachers, or tireless aid workers in war-torn regions, I hope that you will look at them and ask what it is that they have learned from life and how you can learn those same lessons from them.

There are great natural talents, to be sure—Earnhardt at racing, Einstein at science, Daniel Negreanu at poker, Michael Jordan at basketball. But I don't think even they would tell you that success is based on talent, or luck, or good breaks. Thomas Edison famously observed of the scientific success that led others to call him a genius, "Genius is one percent inspiration and ninety-nine percent perspiration." Success is based on your own mental attitude, your own desire, and your own ability to work hard, overcome setbacks, and chip away at smaller goals until the large ones become achievable.

I do not want you to take away from this book the idea that athletes or Buddhists are special people who have tapped into something unavailable to you in your office job, field work, or daily life. On the contrary, the whole point of Buddhism is that enlightenment is available to anyone, dependent only on their will to achieve it. Even if enlightenment is not what you seek spiritually, a calmer, clearer mind and a greater appreciation for life are freely available.

As the quotation at the beginning of this chapter notes, you get to choose how you're going to live. In your internal world—your thoughts, emotions, and attitudes—nobody has the kind of power you do. You are the sovereign ruler, the decider, king or queen of all you survey. Choose to set your attitude according to the very best person you can be, the person you want to be remembered as, or the one you think you could be if you were called upon to be great—the hero in a disaster, the leader when all around are confused and lost. As Joseph Goldstein says, the teachings are simple but they are not always easy. It takes determination and effort, but it can be done.

Thich Nhat Hanh has a wonderful analogy about this readjustment of your mind. Imagine your mind as a garden, he says. The tallest plants are the thoughts and emotional states that you "water" with your attention. They grow tallest and strongest because you are always checking on them, always feeding them. After a while, this process becomes a cycle. When a new situation arises, you look to your mental garden to see what "plant" might be the appropriate one for the situation. But you won't see all the plants equally. You will see the tallest ones first, the ones that you have fed all these years. You might overlook the plant that is actually best for the situation, because it is a small, sickly plant in the shadow of the tall, healthy ones.

Suppose that the tallest plants in your garden look more like weeds than you would care to admit—worry, anger, impatience, resentment. How do you root those out so that they never come back, replacing them instead with blissful, blooming roses of compassion and joy?

You don't. The plants are all a part of you, and if we ripped some out by the root we would be destroying part of our own natural garden. We all feel negative emotions sometimes. The trick is not to get rid of them, but to help the other plants grow equally tall and healthy. Give a little water and attention to joy for a few minutes a day. Think of a situation where you felt compassion, and remind yourself of it now and again, recreating the feelings inside. These "plants" may be small and sickly, but they never die. With a little attention, you can have them growing strong and healthy in a matter of weeks. And without so much of your attention, anger and impatience shrink a little. It doesn't take very long before your garden is balanced again. If you give an extra inch or so to the plants like compassion, joy, and equanimity, they will be slightly taller. It will be their blooms that others see in you, and in a new situation, those will be the plants you see first in your mental garden.

I know plenty of people who will say, "Oh, that's just New Age horseshit. Everybody gets angry when they don't get what they want. Everybody is miserable in bad circumstances." That may be true for many people, but it is not an absolute truth. Athletes, as I have noted, tend to take setbacks philosophically rather than personally, saying, "that's racing" or "that's baseball" rather than losing their emotional balance. Pema Chödrön calls the people who draw wisdom from negative circumstances "spiritual warriors," and she has taught tens of thousands of such warriors. But the strongest evidence that equanimity and joy can be achieved is seen in those people who have suffered greatly and never surrendered their spirits. Martin Luther King Jr., his family, church, and home were targeted, and yet he never lost hope that he was building a better world. He knew others were building it with him, and in his final speech before he was murdered, he said, "I've been to the mountaintop.... I've looked over and I've seen the Promised Land. I may not get there with you. But we, as a people, will get there."[156] He had accepted the possibility (even the likelihood) of his own untimely death, and still he had hope and optimism.

Viktor Frankl survived Auschwitz. In his autobiographical reflection, he observes that when all semblance of civilized humanity had been stripped away in the camps, both from guards and from prisoners, one saw the unguarded attitudes of people, from saints to sadists and everything between. But he never thought that these reactions were immutable, or that they were "the only natural responses" to the hellish circumstances. Instead, the lesson he drew from Auschwitz was this: "Everything can be taken from a man but one thing: the last of the human freedoms—to *choose one's attitude* in any given set of circumstances, to choose one's own way"[157] [italics mine]. If he could take that lesson from Auschwitz, you can certainly take it from your own life.

Mainly, the thing that I most hope you take away from reading *Buddha on the Backstretch* is this: that *you*—no matter who you are—have all the same capacity for great wisdom, great equanimity, and great determination as any of the athletes or Buddhist teachers I've quoted. You can be as brave as Martin Luther King Jr., as tireless a spiritual warrior as Pema Chödrön, and as wise as Viktor Frankl. In fact, the Buddha was an ordinary human being. You have the same capacity for enlightenment as he did. The same jewel that was buried in him—the one that he brought out and polished—is buried in you as well, and it is up to you how much of it you will reveal. One way to begin to reveal it is to ask yourself what will have mattered most to you as you look back on your life. What legacy do you want to leave behind, and what choices must you make, or what actions must you take, in order to build that legacy? Joseph Goldstein writes, "As an experiment, imagine yourself on your deathbed looking back on your life. Imagine it as realistically as you can. What are you holding on to most? What would you have wanted to accomplish in your life? What is of most value to you in those dying moments? The great secret, of course, is to ask those questions now, when we still have time to make creative and meaningful choices."[158] As you come to the end of your reading of this book, I hope you ask yourself these questions, and I hope that you go on making creative, meaningful choices in your life. And as I come to the end of my writing of this book, I leave you with a traditional Buddhist salutation, which signifies "that which is divine in me bows to that which is divine in you." *Namaste.*

Appendix A

How Dale Earnhardt Made Me a Better Buddhist: An Education in Stillness from a Legend of Speed

I may be the only American Buddhist who loves stock-car racing. One doesn't often find common ground between roaring engines and sitting meditation, between the old Confederacy and the *sangha.* But truth and wisdom know no boundaries, and when racing legend Dale Earnhardt was killed in the 2001 Daytona 500, I mourned him both as a race fan and as a Buddhist. For Dale Earnhardt, a tough, cocky southerner, had effortlessly achieved Buddhist ideals that the rest of us practice for years to reach.

Perhaps I should explain a bit about stock-car racing. Although it has flown under the radar of the New York/Los Angeles national media, for millions of Americans it is a consuming passion. It grew in the southern Appalachians, in the 1930s and 1940s, out of a need to soup up one's car to get moonshine past the "revenuers." Moonshiners would boast about their fast cars and challenge each other to races. To avoid the law, drivers had to stay off the streets, so they would race in laps around a field. These fields grew into dirt tracks and eventually into palaces of speed like the Daytona Speedway, which seats nearly a quarter-million people and has grandstands as tall as a four-story building. The drivers grew as well, from moonshiners and car buffs into professional athletes who routinely race with broken bones and still manage to control 3,400 pounds of hurtling metal with just a flick of the wrist.

Dale Earnhardt, forty-nine, was the undisputed ruler of this quicksilver kingdom. Seven times a champion, he was called "The

Intimidator" for his aggressive driving style. He was also called the finest driver ever to turn a steering wheel—with enough daring and talent to squeeze his car into spaces you'd swear a car wouldn't fit (and shouldn't go) and enough competitive fire to bounce his own son off the wall rather than get passed. But when the checkered flag fell, his focused aggression vanished, replaced by a quick wit and a charmingly lopsided grin.

So how did Dale Earnhardt, a devoutly Lutheran southerner, teach me more about Buddhism? I doubt he could answer that question himself—in fact, he'd likely have rolled his eyes at the mention of karma. But I think he would have appreciated the qualities at the heart of Buddhism—self-awareness, presence, compassion, and joy.

Very few of us will ever get to power a race car at speeds approaching 200 miles per hour, much less do it on a weekly basis for twenty years, as he did, but it seems to be an unparalleled means of awakening. On the track, there is nothing but the car and its driver. All the preparation and all the money spent in advance of this moment vanish. The thousands of fans in the stands are invisible, the environment a mere blur. The driver is completely alone, with nothing but his fear, his desire, his passion, and, ultimately, his courage. Not only is your own life in your hands at this moment, but your forty-two opponents' lives as well, for they must depend on your ability to avoid them in a crash.

In such a charged moment, self-deception is impossible. You must know exactly who you are and what you have in you. Drivers facing adversity talk about "digging deep" to find that little bit of inner strength that will carry the day. Earnhardt often had to dig deep, and he had a clear, profound understanding of who he was. Although most southern men of that age are emotionally stoic, he spoke openly about the devastation he felt when his beloved father died. He faced honestly the fact that he had been too busy building a racing career to spend enough time with his children. He spoke of that as one of the only regrets in his life. No excuses, no rationalizations. Just an honest sorrow he could have hidden but didn't.

Racing also forces one to be wholly present during every moment. Driver Kyle Petty once commented that at 200 miles an hour, time itself feels different. Only a person living in the moment could notice that subtle feeling. After a terrible crash at Talladega, Alabama, Earnhardt gave me my most powerful example of bringing presence to even the most painful events. In the hospital the day after the crash, he narrated a taped replay of the accident, which in real time took less than five seconds: "Okay, this first impact here is where my sternum broke. Then I spin, then I get hit again, that wasn't so bad, and then this third one is where my collarbone broke." The room full of reporters sat stunned. Most of the time, drivers have no memory at all of severe crashes. Earnhardt knew which of the dozen or so blows he'd taken had broken which bones, in order. He even closed with a joke about the last car to hit him. (Three weeks later, he climbed into his car, still ashen with pain, and set a new track record.)

He carried that presence off the track as well, in simple ways. Many people spoke of his ability to give his full attention and awareness to a single person even in a room jammed with thousands of people waiting to meet him, to let each and every person feel they'd made a friend. He admitted once that sometimes when he went hunting (a classic southern guy hobby), the gun was ignored—he just wanted to walk in the woods and listen to birds and crickets, fully experiencing the moment before him.

Until his death, Earnhardt's image as "The Intimidator" had kept his compassion hidden. But our authentic self emerges in moments of crisis, and more than once, he leapt out of a wrecked car to make sure his competitors were all right. After his death, it seemed hundreds of people appeared with stories of how he had helped them. It was always done quietly, and he insisted on having no public recognition. Had he been willing to talk about it, he'd have said he was just doing what anyone would do if they could. For me it was proof of his *bodhicitta*, the awakened heart of compassion. In one of his final interviews, Earnhardt showed me more proof. He said, "At the end of the day, I just want everyone to be happy." The interviewer quipped, "Buddy, you're in the wrong business." But Earnhardt merely laughed and repeated himself. Buddhist scholars write pages on the definition of *bodhicitta* and examples of it. But half a world away, in an empty garage, a lanky southerner stretched out his long legs and said gently, "I just want *everyone* to be happy."

When he finally won the Daytona 500, after twenty years of trying (and losing in just about every way imaginable), two extraordinary things happened. First, every single team that competed against him lined up to shake his hand. It had never happened before in motorsports, and it has never happened since. It was a spontaneous outpouring of respect and shared joy, sparked not by the victory, but by the driver's personality. A ferocious competitor but a kind man and a good friend, he made everyone else become better.

Second, when he climbed from the car in Victory Lane, no one would have been surprised if he had taken the moment for himself to savor. But he didn't. Instead, one of the first things he said was, "I hope everyone gets the chance to feel this way just once in their lives." Again, in moments that cannot be rehearsed, we see a person's authentic self, their true nature, and this generosity of spirit was Dale. When I learned to meditate, I learned the practice of universal love—wishing that whatever good arises for me will arise likewise for everyone on earth, and whatever pain befalls me, I alone suffer so that no one else will ever have to suffer it again. No guru taught Earnhardt to be this way—it was simply his nature to bear his defeats with quiet strength and to share his happiness with the whole world.

More than anything, Dale Earnhardt taught me joy. He taught me that when one no longer fears or fights death, then every single moment of life is a precious universe unto itself. Because he risked death every weekend, he loved life all the more, and he lived it at full volume. Twenty years into his marriage, he was still madly, giddily in love with his wife. He glowed with pride whenever any of his children were near. Quiet moments on his farm were a private joy, and with millions of dollars in the bank, he slept with his windows open because he liked to hear the gentle sounds of nature going to sleep and waking up.

I love Buddhism, and I love racing. Wisdom can be found not just in retreats, but in grandstands, with the screams of thousands of race fans deafening you and the roar of engines vibrating through your entire body. Truth lives in both the sacred and the secular, in both speed and stillness. And when you become a student, every person on earth can be a valuable teacher. One of my books says, "Buddha does not always appear as a Buddha. Sometimes he appears…as a woman, a god, a king, or a statesman. Sometimes he appears in a brothel or a gambling house." My Buddha appeared not in robes, but in Wranglers, with twinkling blue eyes and a passion for fast cars. My Buddha died on the final lap of the Daytona 500, on February 18, 2001. Goodbye, Dale, and thank you.

APPENDIX B

Some Buddhist Lists

Buddhism is, for some reason, incredibly fond of lists. Here are some of the key concepts of Buddhism, all in the form of lists. They are arranged by the length of list for no reason beyond my own amusement—there is no traditional order of listing these, and not all paths even use all of them.

The Three Treasures (Taking Refuge)

1. I take refuge in the Buddha.
2. I take refuge in the dharma.
3. I take refuge in the *sangha* (fellow Buddhists, the community of practitioners).

The Four Brahmaviharas (Four Immeasurables)

1. Lovingkindness
2. Compassion
3. Joy
4. Equanimity

The Four Bodhisattva Vows

1. Sentient beings are innumerable; I vow to save them.
2. The fires of desire are unquenchable; I vow to extinguish them.
3. The teachings are limitless; I vow to master them.
4. Nirvana is unattainable; I vow to attain it.

The Five Precepts
1. Not to kill
2. Not to steal
3. Not to commit sexual misconduct
4. Not to speak harshly
5. Not to be intoxicated

The Five Mindfulness Precepts, by Thich Nhat Hanh
A Commentary on the Five Precepts Above

Aware of the suffering caused by death, I vow to cultivate compassion and to protect the lives of people, animals, and ecosystems. I am determined not to kill, not to let others kill, and not to condone acts of violence in the world, in my thinking, and in my way of life.

Aware of the suffering caused by exploitation, social injustice, stealing, and oppression, I vow to cultivate lovingkindness and to work for the well-being of others. I vow to practice generosity by sharing my time, energy, and material resources with those who are in real need. I am determined not to steal and not to possess anything that could be better used by others. I will prevent others from profiting from human suffering or the suffering of other species.

Aware of the suffering caused by sexual misconduct, I vow to cultivate responsibility, and to protect the safety and integrity of individuals, couples, families, and society. I will not engage in sexual relations without love. I vow to respect my commitments and the commitments of others.

Aware of the suffering caused by unmindful speech and the inability to listen to others, I vow to cultivate loving speech and deep listening. Knowing that words can create happiness or suffering, I will speak truthfully, with words that inspire confidence, joy, and hope. I am determined not to spread news that I do not know to be certain and not to criticize or condemn things of which I am not sure. I will make efforts to resolve conflicts arising from miscommunication. I will ask myself before speaking, "Is what I am about to say necessary, kind, and true?"

Aware of the suffering caused by unmindful consumption, I vow to practice mindful eating, drinking, and consuming. I am determined not to ingest foods, or consume images or ideas, that contain toxins or are otherwise negative, wasteful, or destructive, such as certain TV programs, material goods, and conversations. I am aware that to damage my body or my consciousness with these poisons is to betray my ancestors, my society, and future generations. Aware that billions of people lack even the basic necessities of life, I vow to limit my consumption, to think of them when I am consuming, and to support any attempt to distribute the world's resources more equitably.

The Five Hindrances

1. Sensual desire—Craving for pleasure to the senses
2. Anger or ill will—Feelings of malice directed toward others
3. Sloth, torpor, and boredom—Half-hearted action with little or no concentration
4. Restlessness and worry—The inability to calm the mind
5. Doubt—Lack of conviction or trust

The Six Paramitas in Mahayana Buddhism

1. Generosity, giving of oneself (*dana*)
2. Virtue, morality, discipline, proper conduct (*sila*)

3. Patience, tolerance, forbearance, acceptance, endurance (*kshanti*)
4. Energy, diligence, vigor, effort (*viriya*)
5. One-pointed concentration, contemplation (*dhyana*)
6. Wisdom, insight (*prajna*)

The Seven Factors of Enlightenment

1. Mindfulness in all activities and movements both physical and mental
2. Investigation into the nature of dharma
3. Energy (energetic effort, right effort)
4. Joy or rapture
5. Relaxation or tranquility of both body and mind
6. Concentration
7. Equanimity, to face life's vicissitudes with calm mind and tranquility, without disturbance

The Noble Eightfold Path

Generally divided into three parts (wisdom, ethics, and discipline). The word "right" is a translation of *samyañc* (Sanskrit) or *sammā* (Pāli), which denote wholeness, unity, or coherence, and also carry a sense of perfection.

Wisdom (*prajna*)

1. Right View
2. Right Intention

Ethical Conduct (*sila*)

3. Right Speech
4. Right Action
5. Right Livelihood

Mental Discipline (*samadhi*)

6. Right Effort
7. Right Mindfulness
8. Right Concentration

The Sixteen Bodhisattva Precepts

The Three Treasures

1. Taking refuge in the Buddha
2. Taking refuge in the dharma
3. Taking refuge in the sangha

The Three Pure Precepts

4. Do not create evil.
5. Practice good.
6. Actualize good for others.

The Ten Grave Precepts

7. Affirm life—Do not kill.
8. Be giving—Do not steal.
9. Honor the body—Do not misuse sexuality.
10. Manifest truth—Do not lie.
11. Proceed clearly—Do not cloud the mind.
12. See the perfection—Do not speak of others' errors and faults.
13. Realize self and other as one—Do not elevate the self and blame others.
14. Give generously—Do not be withholding.
15. Actualize harmony—Do not be angry.
16. Experience the intimacy of things—Do not defile the Three Treasures.

The Twenty Great Difficulties (and a brief commentary)

1. It is hard for a poor man to be generous.
2. It is hard for a proud man to learn the way of enlightenment.
3. It is hard to seek enlightenment at the cost of self-sacrifice.
4. It is hard to be born while Buddha is in the world.
5. It is hard to hear the teaching of Buddha.
6. It is hard to keep the mind pure against the instincts of the body.
7. It is hard not to desire things that are beautiful and attractive.
8. It is hard for a strong man not to use his strength to satisfy his desires.
9. It is hard not to get angry when one is insulted.
10. It is hard to remain innocent when tempted by sudden circumstances.
11. It is hard to apply oneself to study widely and thoroughly.
12. It is hard not to despise a beginner.
13. It is hard to keep oneself humble.
14. It is hard to find good spiritual friends.
15. It is hard to endure the discipline that leads to enlightenment.
16. It is hard not to be disturbed by external conditions and circumstances.
17. It is hard to teach others by knowing their abilities.
18. It is hard to maintain a peaceful mind.
19. It is hard not to argue about right and wrong.
20. It is hard to find and learn a good method.

Commentary

Good men and bad men differ from each other in their natures. Bad men do not recognize a sinful act as sinful; if its sinfulness is brought to their attention, they do not cease doing it and do not like to have anyone inform them of their sinful acts. Wise men are sensitive to right and wrong; they cease doing anything as soon as they see that it is wrong; they are grateful to anyone who calls their attention to such wrong acts.

BIBLIOGRAPHY

Auguet, Roland. *Cruelty and Civilization: The Roman Games.* London: Routledge, 1972.

Batchelor, Stephen. *Buddhism without Beliefs: A Contemporary Guide to Awakening.* New York: Riverhead Books, 1997.

Beck, Charlotte Joko. *Everyday Zen: Love and Work.* New York: HarperCollins, 1989.

Boyce, Barry. "The Many Faces of the Dalai Lama." *Shambhala Sun* (March 2008) 16,4: 42–49.

Bukkyo Dendo Kyokai (Society for the Promotion of Buddhism). *The Teaching of Buddha.* Tokyo: Kosaido, 1966.

Chah, Ajahn. "Training the Heart." *Buddhadharma: The Practitioner's Quarterly* (Spring 2008) 6,3: 26–31.

Cooper, Andrew. *Playing in the Zone: Exploring the Spiritual Dimensions of Sports.* Boston: Shambhala, 1998.

Dale Earnhardt: Rear View Mirror: Commemorating the Life of the Legend. Sports Publishing, Inc., 2001.

Das, Lama Surya. *Buddha Is as Buddha Does: The Ten Original Practices for Enlightened Living.* New York: HarperCollins, 2007.

Dutton, Monte. *Haul A** and Turn Left: The Wit and Wisdom of NASCAR.* New York: Warner Books, 2006.

The Earnhardt Collection. Chicago: Triumph Books, 2003.

Earnhardt, Dale Jr. *Driver #8.* New York: Warner Books, 2002.

Edelstein, Robert. *NASCAR Generations: The Legacy of Family in NASCAR Racing.* Daytona Beach: NASCAR Publication, 2000.

Epstein, Mark. *Thoughts without a Thinker: Psychotherapy from a Buddhist Perspective.* New York: Basic Books, 1995.

Feldmeier, Peter. "Sex and Spiritual Transformation." *Parabola* (Summer 2007) 32, 2: 68–73. Frankl, Viktor. *Man's Search for Meaning.* New York: Washington Square Press, 1985.

Fussell, Paul. *Thank God for the Atom Bomb and Other Essays.* New York: Summit Books, 1988.

Goldstein, Joseph. *One Dharma: The Emerging Western Buddhism.* San Francisco: HarperSanFrancisco, 2002.

Golenbock, Peter. *American Zoom: Stock Car Racing from the Dirt Tracks to Daytona.* New York: Macmillan, 1993.

Golenbock, Peter. *The Last Lap: The Life and Times of NASCAR's Legendary Heroes.* New York: Macmillan, 1998.

Hagen, Steve. *Buddhism Plain & Simple: The Practice of Being Aware, Right Now, Every Day.* Boston: Charles E. Tuttle Co., 1997.

Inner Frontier. "Equanimity." http://www.innerfrontier.org/Practices/Equanimity.htm.

Jackson, Susan A., and Mihaly Csikszentmihalyi. *Flow in Sports: The Keys to Optimal Experiences and Performances.* Champaign IL: Human Kinetics, 1999.

Jolley, Marc A. *Safe at Home: A Memoir of God, Baseball, and Family.* Macon GA: Mercer University Press, 2005.

King, Martin Luther Jr. "'I've Been to the Mountaintop.' A Call to Conscience: The Landmark Speeches of Martin Luther King, Jr." http://www.stanford.edu/group/King/publications/speeches/I%27ve_been_to_the_mountaintop.pdf.

Kornfield, Jack, editor. *Teachings of the Buddha.* Boston: Shambhala, 1993.

MacGregor, Jeff. *Sunday Money: A Hot Lap around America with NASCAR.* New York: HarperCollins, 2005.

Mack, Joshua. *Karma 101: What Goes around Comes around...and What You Can Do about It.* Gloucester MA: Fair Winds Press, 2002.

McLeod, Ken. "Imagine You're Enlightened." *Buddhadharma* (Fall 2007) 6,1: 32–30.

Menzer, Joe. *The Wildest Ride: A History of NASCAR (or How a Bunch of Good Ol' Boys Built a Billion-Dollar Industry out of Wrecking Cars).* New York: Simon & Schuster, 2001.

Miller, Patrick B., editor. *The Sporting World of the Modern South.* Urbana and Chicago: University of Illinois Press, 2002.

Montville, Leigh. *At the Altar of Speed: The Fast Life and Tragic Death of Dale Earnhardt.* New York: Doubleday, 2001.

Moriarty, Frank. *Dale Earnhardt: 1951–2001.* New York: Metro Books, 2001.

Mumford, Jonn. *Karma Manual: 9 Days to Change Your Life.* St. Paul: Llewellyn Publications, 1999.

Okendzki, Andrew. "Does Buddhism Make You Happy? Debating the Third Noble Truth." *Buddhadharma: The Practitioner's Quarterly* (Spring 2008): 32–41.

Phillips, Benny, and Ben Blake. *Dale Earnhardt: Determined.* Charlotte: UMI Publications, 1998.

Pirsig, Robert. *Zen and the Art of Motorcycle Maintenance: An Inquiry into Values.* New York: HarperCollins, 1974.

Reps, Paul, and Nyogen Senzaki. *Zen Flesh, Zen Bones.* Boston: Shambhala, 1994.

Ricard, Matthieu. *Happiness: A Guide to Developing Life's Most Important Skill.* New York: Little, Brown & Co., 2006.

———. "Why Can't 'I' Be Happy?" *Shambhala Sun* (July 2006): 44–51.

Rich, Ronda. *My Life in the Pits: Living and Learning on the NASCAR Winston Cup Circuit.* New York: HarperCollins, 2002.

Roshi, Taizan Maezumi. *Appreciate Your Life: The Essence of Zen Practice.* Boston: Shambhala, 2002.

Russell, L. D. *Godspeed: Racing Is My Religion.* New York: Continuum, 2007.

Snelling, John. *The Buddhist Handbook: A Complete Guide to Buddhist Schools, Teaching, Practice, and History*. Rochester: Inner Traditions, Ltd., 1991.

Snyder, Eldon E., and Elmer A. Spreitzer. *Social Aspects of Sport: Third Edition*. Englewood Cliffs: Prentice Hall, 1989.

Solomon, Robert C. *Passions: The Philosophy and the Intelligence of Emotions* (audio course). Arlington: The Teaching Company, 2006.

Suzuki, Shunryu. *Zen Mind, Beginner's Mind: Informal Talks on Zen Meditation and Practice*. New York: Weatherhill, 1970.

Thompson, Neal. *Driving with the Devil: Southern Moonshine, Detroit Wheels, and the Birth of NASCAR*. New York: Three Rivers Press, 2006.

Thoreau, Henry David. *Walden; or, Life in the Woods*. New York: Dover, 1995.

Toms, Michael et al. *Buddhism in the West: Spiritual Wisdom for the 21st Century*. Carlsbad CA: Hay House, 1998.

Wallis, Glenn. *The Dhammapada: Verses on the Way: A New Translation of the Teachings of the Buddha with a Guide to Reading the Text*. New York: The Modern Library, 2007.

Willis, Clint, editor. *Why Meditate? The Essential Book about How Meditation Can Change Your Life*. New York: Marlowe & Co., 2001.

Zweig, Eric. *Drive Like Hell: NASCAR's Best Quotes and Quips*. Buffalo: Firefly Books, 2007.

NOTES

[1] Zen Master Dogen, "The Practice of Meditation," in Jack Kornfield, ed., *The Teachings of the Buddha* (Boston: Shambhala Publications, 1993) 159.

[2] Benny Phillips and Ben Blake, *Dale Earnhardt: Determined* (Charlotte: UMI Publications, 1998) 186.

[3] Pema Chödrön, quote in Clint Willis, ed., *Why Meditate? The Essential Book about How Meditation Can Enrich Your Life* (New York: Marlowe & Co., 2001) 211.

[4] Karyn Charles Rybacki and Donald Jay Rybacki, "The King, the Young Prince, and the Last Confederate Soldier: NASCAR on the Cusp," in Patrick Miller, ed., *The Sporting World of the Modern South* (Urbana and Chicago: University of Illinois Press, 2002) 321.

[5] Peter Feldmeier, "Sex and Spiritual Transformation," *Parabola* (Summer 2007): 68.

[6] Neal Thompson, *Driving with the Devil: Southern Moonshine, Detroit Wheels, and the Birth of NASCAR* (New York: Three Rivers Press, 2006) 361.

[7] Jeff MacGregor, *Sunday Money: A Hot Lap around America with NASCAR* (New York: HarperCollins, 2005) 120.

[8] Eric Zweig, *Drive Like Hell: NASCAR's Best Quotes and Quips* (Buffalo: Firefly Books, 2007) 73.

[9] MacGregor, *Sunday Money*, 57.

[10] Paul Fussell, *Thank God for the Atom Bomb and Other Essays* (New York: Summit Books, 1988) 290–92.

[11] Roland Auguet, *Cruelty and Civilization: The Roman Games* (London: Routledge, 1972) 135–36.

[12] Charlotte Joko Beck, *Everyday Zen: Love and Work* (New York: HarperCollins, 1989) 189.

[13] Benny Phillips and Ben Blake, *Dale Earnhardt: Determined* (Charlotte: UMI Publications, 1998) 174.

---

[14] L. D. Russell, *Godspeed: Racing Is My Religion* (New York: Continuum, 2007) 35.

[15] MacGregor, 55.

[16] Ibid., 346.

[17] *Dale Earnhardt: Rear View Mirror: Commemorating the Life of the Legend* (Sports Publishing, Inc., 2001) 21.

[18] John Snelling, *The Buddhist Handbook: A Complete Guide to Buddhist Schools, Teaching, Practice, and History* (Rochester: Inner Traditions, Ltd., 1991) 4.

[19] Steve Hagen, *Buddhism Plain & Simple: The Practice of Being Aware, Right Now, Every Day* (Boston: Charles E. Tuttle Co., 1997) 8.

[20] Joseph Goldstein, *One Dharma: The Emerging Western Buddhism* (San Francisco: HarperSanFrancisco, 2002) 1–2.

[21] Ibid., ix.

[22] I italicize words when they have not become part of the common English vocabulary. Nirvana and dharma have entered the lexicon pretty thoroughly, and so are not italicized.

[23] Glenn Wallis, *The Dhammapada: Verses on the Way: A New Translation of the Teachings of the Buddha with a Guide to Reading the Text* (New York: The Modern Library, 2007) 159. Italics in the original.

[24] Andrew Okendzki, in "Does Buddhism Make You Happy? Debating the Third Noble Truth," *Buddhadharma: The Practitioner's Quarterly* (Spring 2008): 37.

[25] Duane Elgin, *Voluntary Simplicity*, quoted in Clint Willis, ed., *Why Meditate? The Essential Book about How Meditation Can Enrich Your Life* (New York: Marlowe & Co., 2001) 151.

[26] Ken McLeod, "Imagine You're Enlightened," *Shambhala Sun* (Fall 2007): 36.

[27] Ajahn Chah, "Training the Heart," *Buddhadharma: The Practitioner's Quarterly* (Spring 2008): 29.

[28] John Snelling, *The Buddhist Handbook: A Complete Guide to Buddhist Schools, Teaching, Practice, and History* (Rochester: Inner Traditions, Ltd., 1991) 67.

[29] Joseph Goldstein, *One Dharma: The Emerging Western Buddhism* (San Francisco: HarperSanFrancisco, 2002) 102–103.

[30] Ibid., 185.

[31] Henry David Thoreau, *Walden; or, Life in the Woods* (New York: Dover, 1995) 87–88; italics in the original.

[32] Andrew Cooper, *Playing in the Zone: Exploring the Spiritual Dimensions of Sports* (Boston: Shambhala, 1998) 44–45.

[33] Eric Zweig, *Drive Like Hell: NASCAR's Best Quotes and Quips* (Buffalo: Firefly Books, 2007) 15.

[34] Robert Pirsig, *Zen and the Art of Motorcycle Maintenance: An Inquiry into Values* (New York: HarperCollins, 1974) 266.

[35] Ibid., 389–90.

[36] Dale Earnhardt Jr., *Driver #8* (New York: Warner Books, 2002) 44.

[37] Frank Moriarty, *Dale Earnhardt: 1951–2001* (New York: Metro Books, 2001) 13.

[38] Neal Thompson, *Driving with the Devil: Southern Moonshine, Detroit Wheels, and the Birth of NASCAR* (New York: Three Rivers Press, 2006) 355.

[39] Cooper, *Playing in the Zone*, 38.

[40] Susan A. Jackson and Mihaly Csikszentmihalyi, *Flow in Sports: The Keys to Optimal Experiences and Performances* (Champaign IL: Human Kinetics, 1999) 136.

[41] Robert C. Solomon, *Passions: The Philosophy and the Intelligence of Emotions* (audio course) (Arlington: The Teaching Company, 2006).

[42] Jackson and Csikszentmihalyi, *Flow in Sports*, 5.

[43] Ibid., 29.

[44] Matthieu Ricard, "Why Can't 'I' Be Happy?" *Shambhala Sun* (July 2006): 51. Note Ricard's first words in this passage—he is also beginning to hint at the ideal of selflessness, and his next words describe the actions of a selfless person.

[45] Jackson and Csikszentmihalyi, *Flow in Sports*, 27.

[46] Andrew Cooper, *Playing in the Zone: Exploring the Spiritual Dimensions of Sports* (Boston: Shambhala, 1998) 44–45.

---

[47] Eldon E. Snyder and Elmer A. Spreitzer, *Social Aspects of Sport: Third Edition* (Englewood Cliffs: Prentice Hall, 1989) 20. Snyder and Spreitzer describe Maslow's idea of peak experience as including "submersion of the self, self-validating moments, lack of consciousness regarding time and space, wonder and awe, unity of awareness, clarity of perception, loss of anxiety, and a feeling of having been graced," all of which correspond nicely with flow, NASCAR, and Buddhist meditation.

[48] Cooper, *Playing in the Zone*, 119–20.

[49] Jackson and Csikszentmihalyi, *Flow in Sports*, 25–26.

[50] Ibid., 127.

[51] Ibid., 134.

[52] Ibid., 51.

[53] Ibid., 20.

[54] Technically, backup drivers earn points for the owner, but drivers' points determine the championship. One loophole to this rule allows an injured driver to start a race (i.e., take the green flag), then get out of the car and pass the wheel to a relief driver, usually at the first caution flag. Because points are awarded to the man who started the race, this allows the driver to continue to accumulate points. However, it demands that even a seriously injured driver manage to get tightly strapped in and drive at full race speed for as many laps as it takes for a caution to fly, and then do the same week in and week out until he is well enough to resume driving himself.

[55] Ronda Rich, *My Life in the Pits: Living and Learning on the NASCAR Winston Cup Circuit* (New York: HarperCollins, 2002) 219–20.

[56] Patrul Rinpoche, *The Words of My Perfect Teacher*, quoted in Joseph Goldstein, *One Dharma: The Emerging Western Buddhism* (San Francisco: HarperSanFrancisco, 2002) 56.

[57] Goldstein, *One Dharma*, 150–51; italics added.

[58] Bukkyo Dendo Kyokai (Society for the Promotion of Buddhism), *The Teaching of Buddha* (Tokyo: Kosaido, 1966) 262.

[59] Pema Chödrön, *When Things Fall Apart*, excerpted in Clint Willis, ed., *Why Meditate? The Essential Book about How Meditation Can Enrich Your Life* (New York: Marlowe & Co., 2001) 226.

[60] Shunryu Suzuki, *Zen Mind, Beginner's Mind: Informal Talks on Zen Meditation and Practice* (New York: Weatherhill, 1970) 71.

[61] John Snelling, *The Buddhist Handbook: A Complete Guide to Buddhist Schools, Teaching, Practice, and History* (Rochester: Inner Traditions, Ltd., 1991) 55–56.

[62] Steve Hagen, *Buddhism Plain & Simple: The Practice of Being Aware, Right Now, Every Day* (Boston: Charles E. Tuttle Co., 1997) 148.

[63] Lama Surya Das, *Buddha Is as Buddha Does: The Ten Original Practices for Enlightened Living* (New York: HarperCollins, 2007) 30.

[64] Ibid., 78.

[65] Glenn Wallis, *The Dhammapada: Verses on the Way: A New Translation of the Teachings of the Buddha with a Guide to Reading the Text* (New York: The Modern Library, 2007) 112.

[66] Charlotte Joko Beck, *Everyday Zen: Love and Work* (New York: HarperCollins, 1989) 201.

[67] Dale Earnhardt Jr., *Driver #8* (New York: Warner Books, 2002) 23.

[68] Monte Dutton, *Haul A** and Turn Left: The Wit and Wisdom of NASCAR* (New York: Warner Books, 2006) 60; italics added.

[69] *Dale Earnhardt: Rear View Mirror: Commemorating the Life of the Legend* (Sports Publishing, Inc., 2001) 185.

[70] Andrew Cooper, *Playing in the Zone: Exploring the Spiritual Dimensions of Sports* (Boston: Shambhala, 1998) 30.

[71] Ibid., 35.

[72] Das, *Buddha Is as Buddha Does*, 94.

[73] Ibid., xvi.

[74] "The Most Pressure I Ever Faced in Racing Occurred When I Was 15 Years Old," in Benny Phillips and Ben Blake, *Dale Earnhardt: Determined* (Charlotte: UMI Publications, 1998) 33–37.

[75] Steve Hagen, *Buddhism Plain & Simple: The Practice of Being Aware, Right Now, Every Day* (Boston: Charles E. Tuttle Co., 1997) 20.

[76] Michael Toms et al., *Buddhism in the West: Spiritual Wisdom for the 21st Century* (Carlsbad CA: Hay House, 1998) 23.

---

[77] John Snelling, *The Buddhist Handbook: A Complete Guide to Buddhist Schools, Teaching, Practice, and History* (Rochester: Inner Traditions, Ltd., 1991) 6.

[78] *The Earnhardt Collection* (Chicago: Triumph Books, 2003) 207.

[79] Barry Boyce, "The Many Faces of the Dalai Lama," *Shambhala Sun* (March 2008): 46.

[80] Peter Golenbock, *American Zoom: Stock Car Racing from the Dirt Tracks to Daytona* (New York: Macmillan, 1993) 281.

[81] Mark Epstein, *Thoughts without a Thinker: Psychotherapy from a Buddhist Perspective* (New York: Basic Books, 1995) 80–81.

[82] Marc Jolley, *Safe at Home: A Memoir of God, Baseball, and Family* (Macon GA: Mercer University Press, 2005) 61.

[83] Benny Phillips and Ben Blake, *Dale Earnhardt: Determined* (Charlotte: UMI Publications, 1998) 152.

[84] Charlotte Joko Beck, *Everyday Zen: Love and Work* (New York: HarperCollins, 1989) 206.

[85] John Snelling, *The Buddhist Handbook: A Complete Guide to Buddhist Schools, Teaching, Practice, and History* (Rochester: Inner Traditions, Ltd., 1991) 44.

[86] Pema Chödrön, quoted in Clint Willis, ed., *Why Meditate? The Essential Book about How Meditation Can Enrich Your Life* (New York: Marlowe & Co., 2001) 212.

[87] Ibid., 208.

[88] Quoted in Lama Surya Das, *Buddha Is as Buddha Does: The Ten Original Practices for Enlightened Living* (New York: HarperCollins, 2007) 87.

[89] Joseph Goldstein, *One Dharma: The Emerging Western Buddhism* (San Francisco: HarperSanFrancisco, 2002) 111.

[90] Ibid., 104; italics added.

[91] Ronda Rich, *My Life in the Pits: Living and Learning on the NASCAR Winston Cup Circuit* (New York: HarperCollins, 2002) 122.

[92] Robert Edelstein, *NASCAR Generations: The Legacy of Family in NASCAR Racing* (Daytona Beach: NASCAR Publication, 2000) 209.

[93] *Dale Earnhardt: Rear View Mirror: Commemorating the Life of the Legend* (Charlotte: Sports Publishing, Inc., 2001) 191.

[94] Eric Zweig, *Drive Like Hell: NASCAR's Best Quotes and Quips* (Buffalo: Firefly Books, 2007) 65.

[95] Ronda Rich, *My Life in the Pits: Living and Learning on the NASCAR Winston Cup Circuit* (New York: HarperCollins, 2002) 59.

[96] Ibid., 93.

[97] Taizan Maezumi Roshi, *Appreciate Your Life: The Essence of Zen Practice* (Boston: Shambhala, 2002) 55–56.

[98] Eric Zweig, *Drive Like Hell: NASCAR's Best Quotes and Quips* (Buffalo: Firefly Books, 2007) 77.

[99] Taizan Maezumi Roshi, *Appreciate Your Life: The Essence of Zen Practice* (Boston: Shambhala, 2002) 14.

[100] John Snelling, *The Buddhist Handbook: A Complete Guide to Buddhist Schools, Teaching, Practice, and History* (Rochester: Inner Traditions, Ltd., 1991) 7.

[101] Michael Toms et al., *Buddhism in the West: Spiritual Wisdom for the 21st Century* (Carlsbad CA: Hay House, 1998) 53.

[102] Quoted in Joseph Goldstein, *One Dharma: The Emerging Western Buddhism* (San Francisco: HarperSanFrancisco, 2002) 43.

[103] Ibid., 127–28.

[104] Ibid., 186.

[105] Peter Golenbock, *American Zoom: Stock Car Racing from the Dirt Tracks to Daytona* (New York: Macmillan, 1993) 356.

[106] Robert Edelstein, *NASCAR Generations: The Legacy of Family in NASCAR Racing* (Daytona Beach: NASCAR Publication, 2000) 38.

[107] Ibid., 42.

[108] Dale Earnhardt Jr., *Driver #8* (New York: Warner Books, 2002) 94.

[109] Zweig, *Drive Like Hell*, 25.

[110] Ronda Rich, *My Life in the Pits: Living and Learning on the NASCAR Winston Cup Circuit* (New York: HarperCollins, 2002) 87.

[111] Edelstein, *NASCAR Generations*, 45.

[112] Zweig, *Drive Like Hell*, 56.

[113] Jeff MacGregor, *Sunday Money: A Hot Lap around America with NASCAR* (New York: HarperCollins, 2005) 52.

[114] Andrew Cooper, *Playing in the Zone: Exploring the Spiritual Dimensions of Sports* (Boston: Shambhala, 1998) 116.

[115] Charlotte Joko Beck, *Everyday Zen: Love and Work* (New York: HarperCollins, 1989) 10.

[116] Pema Chödrön, *When Things Fall Apart*, excerpted in Clint Willis, ed., *Why Meditate? The Essential Book about How Meditation Can Enrich Your Life* (New York: Marlowe & Co., 2001) 215.

[117] Peter Golenbock, *American Zoom: Stock Car Racing from the Dirt Tracks to Daytona* (New York: Macmillan, 1993) 176.

[118] Quoted in Joseph Goldstein, *One Dharma: The Emerging Western Buddhism* (San Francisco: HarperSanFrancisco, 2002) 47.

[119] Ibid., 52.

[120] Dale Earnhardt Jr., *Driver #8* (New York: Warner Books, 2002) 22.

[121] Golenbock, *American Zoom*, 342.

[122] Robert Edelstein, *NASCAR Generations: The Legacy of Family in NASCAR Racing* (Daytona Beach: NASCAR Publication, 2000) 199.

[123] *The Earnhardt Collection* (Chicago: Triumph Books, 2003) 175.

[124] *Dale Earnhardt: Rear View Mirror: Commemorating the Life of the Legend* (Charlotte: Sports Publishing, Inc., 2001) 22.

[125] Monte Dutton, *Haul A** and Turn Left: The Wit and Wisdom of NASCAR* (New York: Warner Books, 2006) 1.

[126] Inner Frontier, "Equanimity," http://www.innerfrontier.org/Practices/Equanimity.htm (accessed February 24, 2008).

[127] Ibid.

[128] Frank Moriarty, *Dale Earnhardt: 1951–2001* (New York: Metro Books, 2001) 82.

[129] Charlotte Joko Beck, *Everyday Zen: Love and Work* (New York: HarperCollins, 1989) 3–4.

[130] Peter Golenbock, *The Last Lap: The Life and Times of NASCAR's Legendary Heroes* (New York: Macmillan, 1998) 253.

[131] Dale Earnhardt Jr., *Driver #8* (New York: Warner Books, 2002) 76.

[132] Dutton, *Haul A** and Turn Left*, 102.

[133] Ibid., 43.

[134] Ronda Rich, *My Life in the Pits: Living and Learning on the NASCAR Winston Cup Circuit* (New York: HarperCollins, 2002) 70.

[135] Bukkyo Dendo Kyokai (Society for the Promotion of Buddhism), *The Teaching of Buddha* (Tokyo: Kosaido, 1966) 22.

[136] Rich, *My Life in the Pits*, 111.

[137] *Dale Earnhardt: Rear View Mirror: Commemorating the Life of the Legend* (Charlotte: Sports Publishing, Inc., 2001) 65.

[138] Eric Zweig, *Drive Like Hell: NASCAR's Best Quotes and Quips* (Buffalo: Firefly Books, 2007) 78.

[139] Jonn Mumford, *Karma Manual: 9 Days to Change Your Life* (St. Paul: Llewellyn Publications, 1999) 6.

[140] Stephen Batchelor, *Buddhism without Beliefs: A Contemporary Guide to Awakening* (New York: Riverhead Books, 1997) 29.

[141] Peter Golenbock, *American Zoom: Stock Car Racing from the Dirt Tracks to Daytona* (New York: Macmillan, 1993) 13.

[142] Peter Golenbock, *The Last Lap: The Life and Times of NASCAR's Legendary Heroes* (New York: Macmillan, 1998) 155.

[143] Patrick Miller, ed., *The Sporting World of the Modern South* (Urbana and Chicago: University of Illinois Press, 2002) 317.

[144] Golenbock, *The Last Lap*, 183.

[145] Joe Menzer, *The Wildest Ride: A History of NASCAR (or How a Bunch of Good Ol' Boys Built a Billion-Dollar Industry out of Wrecking Cars)* (New York: Simon & Schuster, 2001) 302.

[146] Paul Reps and Nyogen Senzaki, *Zen Flesh, Zen Bones* (Boston: Shambhala, 1994) 122–23.

[147] L. D. Russell, *Godspeed: Racing Is My Religion* (New York: Continuum, 2007) 7.

[148] Ibid., 8.

---

[149] John Snelling, *The Buddhist Handbook: A Complete Guide to Buddhist Schools, Teaching, Practice, and History* (Rochester: Inner Traditions, Ltd., 1991) 19.

[150] 2 Timothy 4:7, King James Version.

[151] Michael Toms et al., *Buddhism in the West: Spiritual Wisdom for the 21st Century* (Carlsbad CA: Hay House, 1998) 87.

[152] Mattheiu Ricard, *Happiness: A Guide to Developing Life's Most Important Skill* (New York: Little, Brown & Co., 2006) 256–57.

[153] Leigh Montville, *At the Altar of Speed: The Fast Life and Tragic Death of Dale Earnhardt* (New York: Doubleday, 2001) 159–61.

[154] Ibid., 179–80.

[155] Joshua Mack, *Karma 101: What Goes around Comes around...and What You Can Do about It* (Gloucester MA: Fair Winds Press, 2002) 79.

[156] Martin Luther King Jr., "I've Been to the Mountaintop," A Call to Conscience: The Landmark Speeches of Martin Luther King, Jr., http://www.stanford.edu/group/King/publications/speeches/I%27ve_been_to_the_mountaintop.pdf (accessed March 8, 2008).

[157] Viktor Frankl, *Man's Search for Meaning* (New York: Washington Square Press, 1984) 86; italics added.

[158] Joseph Goldstein, *One Dharma: The Emerging Western Buddhism* (San Francisco: HarperSanFrancisco, 2002) 33.

INDEX

Alexander, Blaise, 139
Allison, Bobby, 104-105, 135-36
Allison, Clifford, 104
Allison, Davey, 104
Allison family, 4
Aristotle, 25
Auschwitz, 151
Baez, Joan, 148
Baker, Buddy, 113, 114, 132
Batchelor, Stephen, 111, 138
Beck, Charlotte Joko, 14, 69, 96-97, 108, 117, 132
Bristol, Tennessee, race track, 1, 86, 104
Buddhism without Beliefs, 138
buried jewel, metaphor, 112, 151
Burton, Jeff, 10
Chah, Ajahn, 36
chariot racing, 13
Chichester, Sir Francis, 138
Childress, Richard, 95, 131, 142
Chödrön, Pema, 2, 98-99, 101, 108, 118, 145, 150, 151
Chögyam Trungpa Rinpoche, 118
Coleman, Dub, 76
Columbia, South Carolina, race track, 75
Cooper, Andrew, 39-40, 51, 53, 70, 115, 116
Cope, Derrike, 94
Csikszentmihalyi, Mihaly, theory of flow, 46-61; 115
da Vinci, Leonardo, 100-101
Dalai Lama, 24, 89, 111-12
Dallas Cowboys, 4
Daumal, Rene, 120
Daytona 500, 9, 13, 86, 93, 94, 104, 131
Daytona, race track, 8, 57; and restrictor-plate racing, 66-68; 134-35
dharma, 23
Dogen, Zen master, 1, 7
dukkha, 26
Earnhardt, Dale, Jr., 41, 42-43; on mindfulness, 69-70; on pressure, 103; 113; on concentration, 121; on coping with his father's death, 134-35
Earnhardt, Dale: as a racer, 41; gumption, 42; philosophy toward racing, 43; racecar as retreat, 43; preparing for a race, 57-58; going hunting day before a race, 58; driving with a broken back, 60; and restrictor-plate tracks Daytona and

Talladega, 66-68; recollections about growing up (used to illustrate mindfulness), 73-77; letting go of grudges, 88; history at Daytona, 93; assessment of by childhood friend, 118-19; attitude toward accepting loss, 137; quoted in *1000 Paths to Wisdom*, 137; loss of father, 142; on living in the present, 145; contentment with life, 147

Earnhardt, Ralph, story about, 73-77

Edison, Thomas, 148

Edwards, Carl, 133

Eightfold Path, 20-21, 109

Einstein, Albert, 148

Elliott, racing family, 136

emptiness, 27-28

Epstein, Mark, 91

equanimity, defined, 124-25

Everyday Zen, 117

Feldmeier, Peter, 5

flow: defined, 47; racing as a source of, 48; concentration and, 54; control of the self, 54-55; challenges that create best circumstances for flow, 56-57; competing through pain, 59-61

Ford, Henry, 104

Four Noble Truths, 20

Frankl, Viktor, 151

Fussell, Paul, 11

Gant, Harry, 1, 60

Gibbs, Joe, 102

Ginsberg, Allen, 18

gladiator games, 13

Goethe, 111

Goldstein, Joseph, 24, 29, 37-38, 63-64, 101, 120, 149, 151-52

Golenbock, Peter, 139

Grand Canyon, 129

Greenville-Pickens, race track, 74-75

Hagen, Steve, 22, 68

Hammond, Jeff, 122

Hanh, Thich Nhat, 82, 149

Irvan, Ernie, 102

Irwin, Kenny, 139

Jackson, Phil, 100

Jackson, Susan, theory of flow, 46-61

Japan, 129

Japanese religious attitudes, 22

Joe Gibbs Racing, 102

Jordan, Michael, 100, 148

karma, 136

Kerouac, Jack, 18

Keynes, John Maynard, 130

King, Dr. Martin Luther, Jr., 82, 150-51

Kornfield, Jack, 144

Kulwicki, Alan, 103-104, 112-13

Labonte, Bobby, 102

Labonte, Terry, 133

Lama Surya Das, 68, 72, 73

Lombardi, Vince, 100

Lorenzen, Fred, 40
Lotus Sutra, 18, 93, 101
Lund, Tiny, 145
Macbeth, 33
MacGregor, Jeff, 9, 11, 15-16
Mahayana Buddhism, 18, 93
Martinsville, race track, 86
Maslow, Abraham, 51, 52
McLeod, Ken, 35
meditation: basic technique, 34; NASCAR drivers and other athletes practicing, 44
Meister Eckhart, 115
Merton, Thomas, 101
mindfulness: defined, 62; as quality and practice, 64; Zen focus on, 65
monkey mind, 33, 54
Monroe, North Carolina, race track, 75-77
Montoya, Juan Pablo, 4, 10
Montville, Leigh, 146
Mother Teresa, 69
My Life in the Pits, 103
NASCAR: championship points system, 59; driving injured, 59-61;
NASDAQ, 127
Negreanu, Daniel, 100, 148
Neibuhr, Reinhold, 89
New College of Florida, 25
New York Yankees, 4
nirvana, 27
Nobel Peace Prize, 82
observer consciousness (also called witness mentality), 39, 49-51, 109
Oh, Sadaharu, 70-71
paramitas, 94
Pearson, David, 139-40
Petty, Adam, 139, 141
Petty, Kyle, 141-42
Petty, Kyle, 48
Petty, Lee, 140, 141
Petty, Maurice, 141
Petty, Richard, 1, 4, 106, 140
Pirsig, Robert, 42
poker, 7, 148
Posey, Sam, quoted by Paul Fussell, 11
Radner, Gilda, 86, 91
resistance, 108-10
restrictor plates, purpose and use, 57
Ricard, Matthieu, 50-51, 144-45
Rich, Ronda, 102, 103-105, 114, 135-36
Richard Childress Racing, 94
Richmond, Tim, 60
Ripken, Cal, 146
Roman games, 13
Roper, Tony, 139
Roshi, Yasutani, 14
Rudd, Ricky, 60
Russell, L. D., 143
Ruth, Babe, 132
Salzburg, Sharon, 25
samadhi, 53, 55, 115, 117
samsara, 27

Schrader, Ken, 41, 60-61
Sengai, Zen master, 142
Serenity Prayer, 89
Shakespeare, William, 6
Shelmerdine, Kirk, 89
Shinto faith in Japan, 22
Siddhartha Gautama, historical Buddha, 18-20
Siegel, Joel, 86
Snelling, John, 68, 98, 144
Solomon, Robert C., 46
Speedweek, 146
St. Paul, 144
Staunton, Virginia, 126
Stewart, Tony, 41, 86
sukkha, 26
Suzuki, Shunryu, 67-68
Taizan Maezumi Roshi, 105, 107
Talladega, race track, 57; and restrictor-plate racing, 66-68;
Tantric Buddhism, 29
The Teaching of Buddha, 136
Theravada Buddhism, 18
Thoreau, Henry David, 18, 38-39, 111
Tibetan Buddhism, 18
Torre, Joe, 100
Trickle, Dick, 114
Trieloff, Dave, 126, 128
Turner, Curtis, 145
Vickers, Brian, 44-45
Walden; or, Life in the Woods, 18
Wallace, Kenny, 122
Wallace, Rusty, 122
Wallis, Glenn, 30, 69
Waltrip, Darrell, 103, 146-47
Waltrip, Michael, 60, 103, 124
Wide World of Sports, 1
witness mentality (also called observer consciousness), 39, 49-51
Woods, Tiger, 9, 100
Zen and the Art of Motorcycle Maintenance, 42
Zen Buddhism, 18
Zen Flesh, Zen Bones, 142
Zen Mind, Beginner's Mind, 67-68